T0354976

TWO
BOTTLES
OF WATER

TWO BOTTLES OF WATER

JANET FLAUGHER

ARCHWAY
PUBLISHING

Archway Publishing books may be ordered through booksellers or by contacting:

Archway Publishing
1663 Liberty Drive
Bloomington, IN 47403
www.archwaypublishing.com
844-669-3957

ISBN: 978-1-6657-7284-6 (sc)
ISBN: 978-1-6657-7285-3 (e)

Library of Congress Control Number: 2025902218

Print information available on the last page.

Archway Publishing rev. date: 02/21/2025

DEDICATION

For the friends of my heart Julia, Asif, Kristine,
Don, Charlene, and Star. Han hao. Xe xe.

ACKNOWLEDGEMENTS

I want to first thank my husband who filled in some of the gaps in stories when my memories were blurry. I also appreciate the time he spent with me reviewing some of the stories for accuracy and reminding me about others I might have otherwise left out. And of course, I cannot thank him enough to being my partner in the China adventure. He stoically dealt with culture shock and "read" hundreds of Chinese movies on my behalf.

I am also grateful to my family who picked up the threads of our lives and kept everything moving. They took on the care of the family dog, lived in our house, maintained family holiday traditions, to mention some of the larger tasks. They kept us connected to what was happening on the home front. They were in our hearts and heads every day, even at 6,000 miles away.

I would like to acknowledge my friends Dorothy, Maud, and Toni who gave me editing feedback as well as encouragement as the process unfolded. Maud, whose work as a watercolor artist I admire, was also kind enough to take on painting the watercolor covers of the book.

People are what give life its flavor, its purpose, its raison d'etre. I cannot say enough about one very special person, my friend and confidant, Star. Star's devotion, consistency and relentlessness molded my impressions of the China experience. Her dogged focus on helping me become a competent speaker of elementary Mandarin, as well as our frequent "why" conversations provided me with a technicolor vision of the culture I might have missed otherwise. I still remember and review daily the Chinese vocabulary and statements I know and can use properly, intonation included, as a tribute to her kindness and generosity in instructing me about the country she loved. I last saw her in 2010 and last heard from her in 2019 which saddens me. She will always be in my heart.

PROLOGUE

In 2002, I took a job as Head of School at the New School of Collaborative Learning International School in Beijing, China. It was a three-year contract that could be extended indefinitely. I retired from the Greeley Public Schools. My husband quit his job. We arranged for one daughter to live in our condo. Another daughter took our dog. We set up automatic bill-pays. We packed up. We shipped belongings. We moved. We spoke three words of Chinese – ni hao, xe-xe, and wo yao (hello, thank you, I want). We knew Great Wall, Mao, and fortune cookies. We walked into a period of confusion, anxiety, fear, missteps, learning, accepting, engaging, and hard-earned accomplishments. We made some fine new friends, both American and Chinese, and we learned the basics of a new language and culture. And, perhaps most importantly, we affirmed that there is no place like home, no matter how intriguing the place you are living!

We lived in Beijing, China, for a year and a half at the beginning of the century. When I say "we", I speak of myself and my husband. No children – all grown. As you might expect, it was both a fascinating and unsettling experience. We did not speak much Chinese. Unlike the bulk of westerners, we lived in a district of the city that was almost entirely populated by the Chinese. We did not have western stores at our disposal. We were surrounded by Chinese signs and symbols, so for a while, everything we did or bought was based on "best guess". We were the only non-Chinese residents of our apartment complex. Not even the taxi drivers that frequented the taxi stand at the entrance to our complex spoke English.

This memoir recounts my first impressions of our experience. Other's perceptions may differ from mine, but I haven't misrepresented our experience. It was a difficult, confusing, sometimes unfriendly, place for any westerner, and especially for one plunked down in a totally unfamiliar setting, unable to communicate, with a minimal support system. Perhaps expats who lived in more westernized areas of the city enjoyed a life more like that of back home. In spite of all the difficulties we encountered in our stay, I'm glad we did it. It was the experience of a lifetime to be an immigrant and learn firsthand what it was like to be a stranger in a strange land. It also provided great insight into culture shock, unconscious bias (mine), and racism (theirs).

As I was writing, I discovered I needed to use many of the phrases I learned while in Beijing. I have endeavored to share them at the beginning of each chapter, along with their pronunciation and meaning. Note to any linguaphiles, intonation is not added.

CHAPTER 1

Turn On the Lights

Ni hao (knee how) How are you?; Hao (how)
I'm fine; Xe Xe (shay shay) Thank you

April 2002

I HAD WANTED TO WORK IN THE INTERNATIONAL SCHOOL SYSTEM since my father was the Superintendent of the International School of Brussels. In August of 2001, I was hired to be the Head of School for the International School of Quatar. It sounded like an daring situation – living in the American compound; having a driver; wearing an hijab outside the compound; a managerial job with an oil company for my husband, if he wanted it. Compensation and benefits far exceeded what was offered in the U.S.A. I was scheduled to fly to the company's hub in Arizona to sign my contract on September 14, 2001, and we were to depart shortly after. That never happened. 9/11 happened.

After 9/11, there were no flights going anywhere. And even if there had been, we had no intention of going to the Middle East. Let me say that I doubt Quatar had anything to do with the attack. The international school compound was populated with a significant number of Americans, and, of course, expats from many countries. To my knowledge, they had never had issues of terrorism.

On the other hand, there were factors to be considered. Quatar was quite traditional in its cultural views about the role of women. Being responsible and in a leadership position within the compound meant helping expats and their children understand the importance of respecting the cultural norms of the country in which they were a guest.

When tensions are high, as of course they promised to be following the attack on the USA, continuing to affect the appropriate behavior becomes increasingly important. And an attack elicits a patriotic and sometimes defiant response from the victim. One thinks, "They attacked my country. They are the enemy." From my perspective, I was wounded and disappointed as an individual who believes that people are basically good, who believes in getting to know other peoples with the intent to promote cooperation and understanding. I was angry and wanted to consolidate my energies to protect my own. We might be going to war. With that in mind, as an American, I had no place in Quatar. I would be a highly visible target as the head of a school system, and thereby make the school a target. If war were to break out, life in that country might become dangerous.

The central administration was unhappy about my decision, but I still think it was for the best.

I heard about and applied for a Head of School opening in Beijing, China, and for a DOD Superintendency in Okinawa. I applied rather half-heartedly but interviewed for both. Then I was invited to second interviews. The Beijing interview was to take place in China.

I applied for a visa. I took three days off work and jumped on a plane. First to LAX, then to Tokyo; then to Beijing. 12 hours. It was afternoon when we landed, and I walked through the endless, silent, no shops or restaurants, monotone hallways of the Beijing airport concourse with other passengers to reach customs. Standing at the exit was a Board member, Greg, with a large sign that said "Flaugher". He took my bag and we walked to his car. "We've planned a dinner for you. You can meet other Board members and their wives. Tomorrow we'll get in some tourist activities, and then have a meeting with teachers at the school." He maneuvered his compact car through the traffic jams of the ring roads and pulled up at the Lido hotel. The clerks were pleasant. I was able to smile and nod politely. No one spoke English. I knew my 3 words of Chinese. Greg got me checked in and gave me my room key and directions. He would be back for me in an hour, to give me time to change and freshen up.

Room on the 10th floor. Beautiful view of the setting sun. I got out my make up bag and picked an outfit. The lights went out.

I called the front desk. "English?" I asked. Silence, then some unrecognizable Chinese. Cell phones were a new tool. I didn't have one, but I didn't have a number to call Greg, anyway. I opened the drapes as wide as possible, refreshed make-up, changed clothes, and fixed my hair. Still no lights.

I exited my room to find the lights on in the hallway, but I took the stairs, because I didn't want to get caught in the elevator. Greg was waiting. The foyer lights were blazing. Greg was surprised about the room lights.

When I returned to the hotel late in the evening, Greg mentioned to the clerk the problem with the lights. She shook her head, bemused. Upstairs, I opened the door and found my lights back on. By the time I was ready for bed, they were out again. Unbelievable!

Morning came. I showered and dressed by natural light and went about my day. Lights out again in the evening, but I'd anticipated it, so I was prepared.

Much later, after I returned to China to begin my new position, I learned the key card for the room had to be inserted into a slot inside the door to keep the lights burning. When you removed the card, the lights went out. I can't believe I have never seen this in a hotel. I need to get out more!

Interviews with the Board and Spouses

kuaizi (kwhyd-za) chopsticks

As a part of my final interviews for the HOS position, I attended a dinner at a local Chinese restaurant with the School Board. The table was covered by a large lazy Susan, which reached out to about nine inches from the table edge. Our plates, glasses and utensils were placed in that space. The host explained to me that people moved the lazy Susan until an item they wanted to eat was in front of them. Then they used their chopsticks to move some of that dish onto their plate. "Eeww," I thought. "Here I am with a dozen people I do not know, and we are going to be sharing saliva." As if anticipating my discomfort, the host said that for this occasion, serving spoons had been provided. "Good," I thought. I had already been planning how to serve myself and look like I was eating without actually doing so.

Perhaps the most peculiar interview I participated in was with the Board wives. They took me to a Chinese massage parlor, and we all had foot massages while we talked. The ladies were gracious and solicitous to someone who had never done that before, but the masseuse had hands like a body builder. I kept having to ask my hosts to have him go easy on me – much to his delight! He chuckled and clucked throughout the session, but he didn't seem to ease up much. Note to self – I decided massages were off the table in the future! (My husband got a massage to try and help his back not long after we had relocated to China, and I'm pretty sure he got the same guy. He didn't go for a repeat session!)

My hosts shared with me that in the past all masseuses were blind so they could not disclose what people looked like to their enemies. Even in modern day, it was a profession many blind people pursued.

Tour of the School

Xuexiao (shoe-eh-shaow) school; Laoshi (lao-sure) teacher

Day 2 interviews were at the school. I was sitting in the teacher's lounge having lunch with a group of teachers. The food was totally unfamiliar. I was trying not to fumble my chopsticks too badly. One of the teachers stopped to show me how to use them properly. The teachers were a mix – American, Canadian, East Indian, Pakistani, and Chinese. The school was unique in that it taught CSL (Chinese as a Second Language) to the students. Therefore, each classroom had a Chinese teacher teaming with the American/International one. And every child took CSL. In addition, those students who needed to learn English took ESL. Two of the staff took me on a tour of the school, which mirrored what a school in the States would look like. The bathrooms, however, were quite a surprise. After being knocked over by the foul smell, you had to squat over the wall of a kind of cement trough. I wondered if we could have something more Western installed. (I knew from my hotel that regular bathrooms existed.) My tour guide shared that the school was moving to another location over the summer, and I made a note to ask the Board if we could negotiate for bathrooms with toilets.

Initially, the teachers were subdued, but I had lots of questions. It wasn't long before we were engaged in lively conversation. Then, suddenly, they began to tell me about the things they needed to improve the school. I began to make a list. At the end of the interview, I promised to share their list with the Board Chair.

The students at NSCL were from many countries – USA, England, Armenia, France, Australia, Japan, Korea, and New Guinea, to name a few. And there were a few Chinese students. They were the children of the Chinese teachers. Normally, Chinese children were not allowed to go to "foreign" schools, but an exception was made for these to make it easier on the working mothers. Students addressed their teachers politely – name followed by Laoshi, such as, Smith Laoshi, or Teacher Smith.

Three days after I returned to the States, the NSCL Board Chairperson called me and offered me the position, to begin in July. I accepted. I withdrew from candidacy at the DOD schools. And the great adventure began!

CHAPTER 2

From Denver to Paris, China

Ni chi le ma? (knee chur la ma?) Hello/have
you eaten?; Wo shi (wah sure) I am; Zai nar
(z-eye nar) bathroom

WE BEGAN OUR CHINA ADVENTURE IN THE SPRING OF 2002. WE
boxed up all the clothing, toiletries, household basics, pictures,
and reminders of home we thought we would need for our
initial 3-year stay. All the boxes were labeled and mailed to
the New School of Collaborative Learning (NSCL) in the
Haidian District of Beijing, China. We put our bills on auto pay.
One daughter volunteered to take the dog. Another daughter
volunteered to live in our townhome. I resigned from my
position as Principal at the area charter school and Bill quit his
job with the County. We flew to Beijing in late June with two
suitcases, two carry-ons, and a handful, or in this instance a
mouthful, of Chinese words. xe xe, hao, ni hao, ni chi le ma, zai
nar, wo yao, wo shi. Denver to LA, LA to Tokyo, and Tokyo to
Beijing. About 12 hours in the air, plus stopovers.

We discovered on that first day in June how hot and humid Beijing was in the summer. The temperature was 96 and the humidity matched it. We exited the airport terminal to a warm rain shower. We spent that entire first summer feeling damp the minute we walked out our door. Air-conditioned buildings were a blessing – our apartment, the school, and the embassy.

My Board member contact, Greg, picked us up at the airport and took us to our new home on Xi San Qi Road. The Fang Dan Li Shu (Fontainebleau Apartments) in the Haidian district was modeled after Paris, France. In the main Tuilleries courtyard, one could sit by the koi pond and enjoy a view of less-than-scale models of the Eiffel Tower, the Champs Elysée and the Arc de Triumph. The apartments were posh, upscale and large. Our home was a corner, first floor apartment. It had two bedrooms, two bathrooms, a living/dining area, a kitchen, an entry and an enclosed (though unheated) sunroom. The buildings were two stories high, so we had occupants in the apartment above us. Our French doors opened onto a small patio and a well-kept grassy area. As long as we lived there, I rarely saw anyone tending the grounds, yet everything was immaculate and lush.

We also had a door man. He was a young fellow probably in his early twenties dressed in a military uniform who stood at our building's front door and opened it to let us in. Often, when we returned from grocery shopping, he would help us carry groceries inside. That was particularly nice during the long, cold winter. His English was as meager as my Chinese. I assumed he was there all day long, although we were not, but I couldn't ask whether he got a lunch break. He was there when we left for work and there when we returned home. He was not there at night and was only there intermittently on the weekends.

Our apartment was furnished by the school, and the furniture was acceptable, with two exceptions. The card table and four folding chairs in the dining area had to go. I talked with the Board, and they were replaced with a decent dining set. The mattress in the master bedroom had broken springs, and after two weeks of miserable and painful sleep, it, too, was replaced.

The kitchen was supplied with basic dishware, silverware, pots and pans, and salt and pepper. We were ecstatic to see our shipped boxes neatly stacked in the spare bedroom, since it meant we had linens, pillows, and blankets, as well as towels and additional clothing.

By the time the Board member took us to the grocery store to buy staples on that first day, it was getting late. The Shao Bai Yan (Little White Goat) was a neighborhood market. We were, of course, the only westerners. We filled our basket with basics, milk, butter, bread, eggs, vegetables, fruit, and meat. We discovered the words for ice cream - Bing Qi Ling – and purchased some. The bread was particularly interesting. It came in cubes. Each slice of bread was a perfect square. The squares were packaged together in a plastic bag in a perfect cube. Different, but excellent tasting. We were quick to discover although we had bread, we had no toaster.

The next day, our contact picked us up in the morning and took us to IKEA for sundries. It was such a surprise to see a western store in China, but It was a delight to find items familiar to western tastes. And we did find a toaster. We went to IKEA several times; I think just because it felt comfortable and the restaurant was easy to negotiate and had familiar food. We have an IKEA near us in the States, but we have never shopped there.

Later in the day, he took us to the black market to buy phone cards so we could make international calls at a discount rate. We would key in the number on the card and be able to call the states and talk to our families until the minutes on the card ran out. We were regular black market phone card customers after that, and later, when, as Head of School, I welcomed new staff to Beijing, I made sure my staff included phone cards with clear instructions for use and how to replenish as part of new staff welcome packages.

After that, we were on our own. We were planful. If we needed to go somewhere, I would ask my secretary ahead of time to write it down on a slip of paper I could share with a taxi driver. Generally, we walked to the corner of our complex and took a taxi, since they were very cheap. I could ride from my school to meetings at the Embassy, ISB, or AMCHAM for about $5. Buses were available, but always crowded. The Light rail - qing gui- (ching guay) went to the downtown area and to the Canadian Embassy, where my husband worked, but to get to the Haidian station, one had to take a taxi or the bus. It was a great distance from our apartment complex. Later, a qing gui (ching guay) station opened nearer our home, but still required using a taxi or bus. Taxis did not like to get a fare that only wanted to go a short distance, so that presented a problem. There were "black" taxis, but you could not find them at nice residences. The government-sponsored taxi drivers would run them off. They could be found at the qing gui (ching guay) station near our home, so Bill often came home in one.

Apartment Living

Fung Dan Li Shi (fung dan lee sure)
Fontainebleau Apartments; San huan lu (San
Juan Loo) Third Ring Road; Xi San Qi (She
San Chi) West 3rd Ring Road; Laoai (laow
eye) – foreigner, foreign devil

Our apartment complex, Fung Dan Li Shi (The Fontainebleau), was located on Xi San Qi (Third Ring Road), and was beautiful by any standards. It mimicked traditional continental architecture. There was a guarded gate. You could walk in, but taxis and visitors were screened at the gate. When you entered the complex, you drove or walked down the "Champs Elysses". At the end were a miniature Eiffel Tower and Arch de Triumphe. The gardens (Tuileries, I guess) were meticulously maintained. The apartment buildings had two floors, and each contained 4 spacious apartments. Ours was about a quarter mile from the main gate. We were on the first floor and opened onto the gardens on the south and the east. Our front door faced west, and to our north, across the inner foyer, was the other main floor apartment. There was an elevator to the second floor.

When you walked through our front door, you stepped into a foyer. There was a bathroom on the left and a bedroom on the right. Moving forward, you walked past the refrigerator and into the kitchen. If you turned to the left before you entered the kitchen, you walked into the dining and living area. At the end of that large room there were French doors leading into another room. At first, I thought it was a sunroom, but it wasn't long before I learned its true purpose. To the left of the living room was a door that opened into the master bedroom/bath. On the right side of the living room were French doors that led outside to a very large yard and the famous Beijing Kennel Club, which I will discuss later. The floors were all ceramic tile, and a plethora of windows gave the apartment a bright and welcoming atmosphere. The rooms had overhead lights only, except for the living room. The living room had a table lamp and a floor lamp.

We had a door man. He was a very young gentleman – probably around 18-19. He wore a uniform with a helmet that reminded me of a British grenadier. He was there most days, although sometimes I thought he played hooky because his post was unmanned. He was always pleasant but reserved. Maybe he was a spy assigned to report on what the "foreign devils" (laowai) were doing. The building was air-conditioned. There was a color television. There was a washing machine. Our mailbox was right outside our front door. Lovely.

As we settled in, we began to notice and learn to adjust to the cultural differences.

A Chinese Kitchen

Wo chi (wa chur) I eat; Ni chi le ma? (ni chur la ma) Have you eaten? (This is actually a way of greeting people. During Mao's time in power, 30 million Chinese starved to death. When people met, they were trying to assist those who needed food, hence the greeting.)

We would expect kitchens to be pretty much the same all over the world. Not so. My kitchen had a two-burner gas stove top. There was no oven. The Chinese are not big bakers. A lot of their pastries are steamed. The counters on the stove side of the kitchen were normal enough. However, on the sink side of the kitchen, the sink was at the normal level while the rest of the counter was about 10 inches lower. It was too low to comfortably work at, but just a bit too high to use as a bench. For me. It was lost space, and my cooking work area was significantly diminished. All this was manageable, though crowded.

However, when we opened the cupboard under the sink, we were overwhelmed by the stench. The drainpipe from the sink was stuck directly into the sewer pipe that exited the house. There was no trap (required on American plumbing.) And the cupboard smelled like raw sewage. Ok. We decided we just wouldn't ever open those doors again. Unfortunately, cupboards are not airtight. The other lower cupboards exuded the same pungent odor. So, the lower cupboards were off limits. Our staples were kept in the overhead cabinets along with dishes and pots and pans that had been provided to us. It was actually a shame to lose the cupboard space, as there were no cupboards anywhere else in the apartment. The drainpipe was also a problem. More than once, it split just as I was draining the sink. I was standing in a puddle of water each time. Repairmen had to be called to fix the pipe, which they happily did. We always wondered why they didn't at least tape the pipe where it dove into the sewer pipe, but that never happened. And, at least, the sewer never backed up! Strike one for Chinese plumbing!

The refrigerator was different. It stood just outside the kitchen in the foyer. It looked like a miniature airstream camper, standing up on its end. It stood about 5 feet tall in it's stocking feet! The freezer was the size of a small microwave (did I mention there was no microwave?), with no ice cube trays (I found some at IKEA.) so it didn't hold much. We didn't shop everyday like our Chinese hosts, so the fridge and freezer were always packed full.

Not having an oven was a challenge, but one day when grocery shopping, we happened on a tiny toaster oven, which we triumphantly purchased. When we got it home, we realized it was so small we didn't have any pots or pans that fit inside. On another shopping trip, we found a four-cup casserole and bought it. When we went to the states for Christmas, I purchased a baking sheet for a child's play kitchen. It was still too big, but Mr. Xin cut it down enough that we could make a batch of 6 cookies. We also taught ourselves how to make bagels and toast them by pairs in the oven.

This is the Way We Wash Our Clothes

Xiyi dian (she yee dian) Laundry

The washer was another frustrating experience. We named it the Knot-mobile. It looked like a regular washer, but it had no middle section in the tub. Clothes were churned around into a giant wet knot, that took strength and patience to untangle. It also had a hot water and a cold-water intake valve which had to be turned on and off before and after washing, and both had to be on or off. There were no cold-water washes.

Another interesting feature of the washer was that it emptied out onto the entryway floor in which there was a drain. So, when the washer was running, you would have to wade to the guest room, kitchen, or the guest bathroom. And when the wash was done, you got to wash the floor, which was covered with lint. Being a resourceful American, I conferred with my facilities manager and carefully explained how a little remodeling could run the drain through a pipe to hook up with the bathroom shower drain. He assured me it would not be a problem to fix.

The remodeling was done while we were out. A gaping, jagged-edged hole was drilled into the wall between the foyer and the bathroom, and a long flexible plastic pipe went through that hole and onto the bathroom floor. Problem solved! I had anticipated they would go under the floor to adjust the plumbing, but I was totally wrong. In fact, now that I think about it, I don't know if there ws anything under the floor but dirt. Now the washer drained all over the bathroom floor. From then on, the bathroom was off limits when the knot-mobile was running. Strike two!

The Sun Room.

I really thought this room was going to be wonderful in the winter. I had visions of sitting out there and reading and watching my neighbors. We just needed to get rid of all the paraphernalia hanging from the ceiling and folded against the walls. That was not to be. The paraphernalia were actually clotheslines that raised and lowered from the ceiling. The items leaning against the walls were clothes racks. Our apartment had a washing machine, but no dryer. Unbelievably, that was the norm. People hung their clothing up to dry – inside. I learned in time that the room was also unheated. In the dead of winter, we would hang up clothes and leave them for hours and hope they would eventually dry. I remember bringing in stiffly frozen jeans to see if they were wearable.

Bathrooms

Zai nar (tzeye nar) bathroom

My husband noticed the bathrooms were generally smelly. He discovered the toilets had a pipe that threaded directly into the drainpipe (no trap) that exited the house, and the bowls were not sealed down to the floor. They moved around! We sat on them gingerly and took our chances. In addition, the master bathroom had a very fancy shower/tub with wall and tub jets. However, none of the bells and whistles worked. You could run a bath or stand under the shower. That was it. And the sides of the tub were quite high, like about 3 feet. For a shortie, like me, just getting into the tub presented a challenge, and getting out was even harder! You could use a step stool to get in, but there was no stool to help you get out. I often took a shower in the guest bath, which was another interesting adventure.

The guest bathroom presented another challenge. There was a raised rectangle on the south floor of the room– probably 4 x 6. There was a shower nozzle and water valves. There was no shower wall or door, no shower curtain. There was no medicine cabinet or shelves or cabinets for towels and toiletries. The first time I used it, my clothes and towels, toilet and sink, make-up, brush and comb, and hair drier were as wet as I was. After that we purchased a small shelf and put it outside the bathroom door. It worked fine for keeping belongings dry but was not great for privacy and convenience. I guess it was a great way to get rid of unwanted guests! Anyway, that was strike 3 for Chinese plumbing!

The Bedrooms

Woshi (Wah she) Bedroom; Chuang (She-ang) Bed; Chuang dian (She-ang dee ahn) Mattress

The master bedroom was large, with a closet that ran almost the length of one wall. The bed was a king, and yet there was plenty of room for nightstands, chairs, and dressers. I woke up after our first night there with bruises up and down the right side of my body. The mattress had broken springs which pressed into me all night. We flipped the mattress, but the second night was just as bad as the first. Until we were able to get a new mattress, I slept on the couch.

I could have slept in the guest bedroom, but for some reason I didn't. It was a pretty, sunny little room that faced the front of the building. It had a nice closet and dresser, which we used to store extra clothing and junk.

The Living Area

Keting (Kuh ching) Living Room

The living room was our safe area. It was tiled. It had large windows on two sides. It always felt light and airy. It had a large, overstuffed leather couch and matching chair. They were familiar, and comfortable. When you sat down, you were engulfed and surrounded. We had end and coffee tables. And a television. And a large fixture that was the air conditioner/ heater sitting in one corner.

The dining room table with 4 chairs was problematic. I'm not sure who decorated the apartment, but we let my business manager know right away that a card table and four folding chairs were not suitable, and they were replaced by an oak set that could seat eight. Much better!

We spent many cozy hours watching pirated videos of our favorite movies in our living room. You could buy the videos anywhere from hawkers on the streets for about a dollar. Some were even good quality. Many, however, were not. One named the stars of Pay it Forward as Kevin Spacer and Helen Hand. I remember in the middle of another film; we watched someone get up from a front row seat and walk across the screen! Hysterical! Sometimes you could hear mumbling in the background. The absolute wildest was Signs. The whole movie had a green tint.

Bill also watched a lot of television while he was waiting to start his job. There was a movie channel. I don't believe there were any western movies. The movies were in Chinese but had subtitles in English and Korean. He always says he "read" a lot of movies while we were in China.

The Beijing Kennel Club

Wo shi Meguoran (Wah sure Mei guo ran) I am an American

We had no pets while we were in China. We left our old Samoyed, Luna, with our children, who were kind enough to care for her. But we discovered the residents of Beijing had recently become enamored with having dogs. Everyone had a dog that they loved and pampered.

The city was mostly apartments, so every day Beijingers walked their dogs. And in our apartment complex, for some reason never discovered by me, our yard was the gathering place, the dog park, if you will, for Fung Dan Li Shi residents and their pets.

Every morning, a dozen or more dog owners (usually female) gathered outside our window to have a smoke and let their dogs run around our yard. Every evening it was the same. Although some days the smell of smoke became overpowering, there was no problem with dog poop. The dog owners faithfully cleaned it up and carried it away.

Our efforts to interact with the group (I called them the "Beijing Kennel Club) were met with what I would equate to anxious, if not horrified, faces. We backed off. We were the only Westerners in the complex. Our Chinese was minimal, as was their English. And of course, the Chinese were still quite suspicious of Americans. It was several months before the Beijing Kennel Club members acknowledged our existence, usually with a curt nod and a suspicious glance if we happened to pass by.

CHAPTER 3

Figuring it Out, "Say, what?"

An Unsettling Health Examination

Bu hao (boo how!) bad, very bad!

PRIOR TO BEGIN GIVEN A VISA TO LIVE AND WORK IN CHINA, MY husband and I had to complete an extensive physical examination and present the results to the Chinese government. We did so and were cleared in all areas. Upon arriving in Beijing, we were informed by the school's Business Manager that we had to submit to a health examination at the Chinese Department of Health to confirm we were fit to stay in the country. We questioned the need for this examination, as we had been required to have a complete physical and be up to date on all vaccinations prior to getting a visa to China. Our records had been provided.

Nevertheless, on a hot, humid, July morning, carrying our health information with us, Bill and I were transported to an imposing government building. We had a note in Chinese we presented to the staff, and we were whisked off to examination rooms. No one spoke English. Everyone was completely serious, no welcoming atmosphere, no smiles. It was indicated we should disrobe and dress in the hospital gowns that were provided. We were moved from room-to-room, weighed and measured, temp taken, eyes, ears, throat, body checked, treadmill test, etc. In one room, I recall getting an injection before I could object. I have no idea what the shot was, and I never was able to discover the answer, no matter how many people I talked to about it. It was hot and muggy in the building and the waiting time in each room was long, although there was a dearth of customers. I was tired and really upset by the injection.

In the final room, the health staff approached me with supplies to take blood. I refused, and continued to refuse until the staff left the room. You could say I threw a fit, because I did! I didn't want some stranger in a place I didn't feel was completely trustworthy, where I didn't even know how sanitary it was, poking me with needles. Unconscious bias? Absolutely! I was responding from my personal belief system about China. Sometime later, someone who spoke English came into the room and told me I did not have to give blood and I could get dressed and go to the waiting room. Later I found out they had called the Business Manager, who had managed to talk them out of the blood test.

Bill and I both passed muster (again) and received a government certification of our fitness to work in China. I have to say, we felt completely violated by the activity, and we were new enough to our environment to entertain the thought of bailing on the whole China experience. But calmer heads prevailed. My Board Chair and other members apologized profusely for the situation we had been subjected to and assured us we were in no danger.

Oppressive Heat and Bone-chilling Cold

Wo hen leng (wa hun lung) I'm cold

When we moved into the apartment, we were told the pot-bellied stove-looking fixture in the living room was our air conditioner. It was wonderful and we never suffered from the oppressive Beijing summer heat. When October came, it began to get cold. There were no heating thermometer controls in the apartment. My secretary inquired for me as to how we were to get heat, and she was told it would be turned on by the apartment management in November and off in April.

It snowed. We were freezing. I hoped it would be warmer at work, but the same scenario presented itself, so I was cold all day and cold all night. Bill and I weren't used to having no control over our creature comforts. I complained to my Board Chair, and he came over. He was very apologetic. The air-conditioner was also a heater. All the information/directions were presented in Chinese, though, so we had no idea. He showed us how to turn on the heat. From then on, we were warm at home when we wanted to be. Businesses, including schools, waited until November, however. Until then, our staff and students dressed warmly and wore coats.

Paying the Utilities

Renminbi (rem em bee) money/currency;
Yuan (you ahn) Dollar(s)

In December we got a notification in the mailbox that looked important. I took the notice to school and my secretary translated it and told me we needed to go pay our heating bill. I called my Board contact and found out what needed to be done. It wasn't anything easy, like sending a check or paying by credit card on a website. First of all, the Chinese didn't use checks and credit cards were a very new thing and few companies used them. Everything was cash and carry. Secondly, you had to go in person to pay the bill. So one of the Board members came to the complex and picked my husband up to go pay the bill.

They drove to what seemed to be a bank/post office sort of set up. They went to the counter and presented the notice and a stack of yuan. The clerk took the amount of money needed and stamped the notice. While they were standing there, a couple stepped up to the window next to them and handed over a suitcase filled with cash. Bill was in shock at seeing such a large sum of money. Later we learned more about how purchases were made in China. People paid cash, even for cars and houses. It was suggested that the couple was probably making a payment on the house they were going to buy. We thought it was extraordinary that people walked around carrying huge sums of money in a city of 14 million people without a worry.

(While we were there, the exchange rate was about 600 yuan to one dollar.)

Interestingly, Beijing was a relatively safe environment. The average citizen was fearful of the government. They were cautious not to get crossways with the authorities. Tickets and warnings were not the way infractions were addressed. If you did something illegal or even questionable, you were just hauled away. And some people never returned. So, we were not afraid to go about our business in the day or the evening. There was really no threat of being mugged or assaulted, and no one ever accosted or threatened us during our stay.

The Clumps Upstairs

Linju (lynn chew) Neighbor

Not long after we moved in, we became aware of the family above us. Not because they introduced themselves (everyone in our complex steered clear of us), but because it sounded like they were rolling bowling balls across the floor every day. Or maybe their young child was roller skating. It could have been they were walking around in wooden shoes. Whatever it was they were doing, we named them the Clumps.

The Clumps were active during the day and quiet at night. There was no help for the day noise, but we were grateful they were quiet at night. Never once did we see them, so we could never give them the once over, to see if they were wearing Dutch hats and wooden shoes, or what their matching bowling bags looked like - long straps to swing them over the shoulder or two straps to secure them safely on the back. Did the child's bag fit into a stroller, or roll behind on tiny wheels? Our imaginations ran wild with endless possibilities.

To make matters worse, the Clumps started a remodeling project soon after we moved in. What sounded like jackhammers jarred the building all day long! For several weeks! We never did learn what they were doing, but after the project ended, we still had the bowling balls (Maybe they installed an actual bowling alley!)

Ordering Water

Wei? (way) Hello; Wo yao er tong shui (Wah yow are tongue schway) I want two bottles of water

Neither I nor my husband knew much about China prior to moving there. We did some research to learn what to expect, what everyday life was like, how to use simple phrases in Chinese. We were basically immigrants, but the international school environment would be western/American, so we had a home base. The staff would be English-speaking. Until my husband found a job, he could volunteer at the school and we could enjoy a "western" lunch every day.

We quickly discovered that potable water for cooking and drinking had to be ordered in bottles. We did not drink from the sink. When we moved in, there were 4 5-gallon bottles in our apartment along with a dispenser. We were given the phone number of the local delivery company. My secretary taught me the numbers from one to 10 – yi, er, san, si, wo, liu, qi, ba, jiu, shi. She taught me to say I want – wo yao. One morning in July when our store of water was nearing depletion, we put on our grown-up hats and made our first attempt at placing an order. I picked up the phone and dialed the number. "Hwai," said a voice at the other end. I took a deep breath. "Wao shur Janet Flaugher. Wao yao er tong shui. Xi San Qi, Fung Dan Li Sheu." "Pretty good, I thought! There was a long silence at the other end of the line. Then finally muted laughter. And a voice said,

"Hao, hao, ok," and the line went dead. Mortified, we waited to see whether my order had been understood.

Twenty minutes later our bell rang. We opened the door to a short, 100-pound man in a blue cotton shirt, military green shorts, and flip flops, with two 5-gallon bottles on his shoulders. He smiled and bobbed his head, and we bobbed back, "Ni hao." He put the bottles next to the dispenser and gestured that he would take the other bottles away with him. We agreed. We gave him some yuan – a tip. He frowned and shook his head, then took it when we insisted. He picked up the other bottles and left. Success! We later learned the school was regularly billed for our water, so there was no cost to us.

From that day on, every two weeks or so, I placed my order for two bottles of water. By my third order, the voice as the other end of the line said "ok, ok, ok, "before I'd finished saying my piece; sometimes the moment I said my name. I always wondered if it was because they hated hearing me butcher the language.

We often saw water delivery men out on the streets. They pedaled blue three-wheeled bicycles (isn't that an oxymoron?) with a miniature metal truck bed mounted over the back wheels. The bed could fit several bottles of water. The men wore the same uniform as our delivery man, although in winter the shorts were exchanged for long pants, and padded coats covered all. They were typically very small, slightly built, with calves the size of the Hulk's. We learned later that tips were frowned on, so we refrained from tipping our waterman after that first time.

Reading Television

Dianshi (Deeann Sure) Television

Our apartment was equipped with a television. It was modern enough for the time – color, remote channel changer, dvd player. It had many channels, the majority of which were in Chinese. Most news came from Beijing news channels. There was a European channel, which was largely dedicated to sporting events – soccer and bike racing. There was a news channel in English, controlled by the Chinese government. There were movie channels – all in Chinese. But the movie channels also had subtitles in English. We spent many evenings - and my husband many days, until he became employed at the Canadian Embassy (Janada da si guan) - "reading" kung fu movies.

On a trip to the Pearl Market (Hong Chao), we discovered street hawkers with dvd's of popular movies and television shows in English. They cost about a dollar. They were pirated, of course. We purchased a couple to try them out and our initial experience was fantastic. We purchased more, and we discovered there were different levels of quality. Everything in the movie "Signs" was green. One dvd cover promoted Helen Hand and Kevin Spacer. In the middle of one movie, a person in the front row got up and walked across the screen to the aisle. Hysterical! But it was pirated dvd's or reading television, so the choice was an easy one. We did try other forms of entertainment as time went by. We went to see the tourist sites – the Great

Wall at Badaling; Tiananmen Square; the Ming Tombs, the Peiking Man site; Chinese Opera – but tv was there every day. We did manage to find all the seasons of X Files, which kept us going for quite a while.

The Internet Connection

Diannao (deeann now) Computer

In addition to television, people could get on computers. We did not have one, but sometimes Bill came to volunteer at the school and on those days he was able to use a PC. Internet was monitored by the Chinese government and sometimes it was impossible to get information. The Chinese frequently blocked channels, denying that it was going on and blaming it on poor connections. My teachers at the school often complained bitterly about the practice. In fact, when SARs started, we knew virtually nothing about it for months. We first heard about it when we were in the States for Christmas. It took a lot of pressure from entities outside of China to get the country to open up and tell the populace what was going on.

We did not have a computer or laptop at home. Nor did we have smart phones. My computer at the school was "cleansed".

Foods I Never Thought of Eating

*Dasuan (da sueann) garlic; Suan (Sueann)
garlic leaves; tudo (too doe) potato; qiezi
(chi ed za) eggplant; gan bian si ji do (gone
beyon c g doe) green beans sauteed in oil and
garlic; joudza (jow dza) dumplings; Wo chi
(Wa chur) I eat*

The time I opened my lunch at school and found cuttlefish pizza with mushrooms was not so pleasant. I like some seafood – salmon, halibut, sea bass, shrimp – but I don't like to prepare it. I do NOT like octopus or squid. Until I came to China, it never even occurred to me to put fish on pizza! But Beijing had a Pizza Hut restaurant. And cuttlefish was a fan favorite. It still gives me the chills just thinking about it. Ugh!

My secretary regularly ordered my lunch from the restaurant that provided the primary school's meals on Tuesdays and Fridays. Tina knew from the time she ordered me cuttlefish and mushroom pizza, about things to avoid. I often opened the Styrofoam container and saw slices of meat, chunks of what looked like potato, and eggplant (qiezi) swimming in oil. One section might be filled with a cooked dark green vegetable that looked like spring onion tops. I came to know it was garlic tops from past experience. And they were delicious. None of the bite of garlic cloves. They were mellow with the faintest hint of garlic. I could buy them at Shao Bi Yan when I went for lettuce. I could also buy fresh green beans.

Since canned and frozen items were not readily available, I always cooked fresh veggies. The beans were remarkable, and not just because they tasted good. They were also incredibly long - typically between two and three feet. They were nicely rolled up and packaged. We would wash them and chop them into bite size pieces to cook. I bought small eggplant shaped like sweet potatoes to chop and add to stews and soups and stir-frys.

I didn't buy, but had unwittingly eaten, chicken feet, horse meat, seaweed, red bean paste, fish heads and winter melon. I didn't buy the crabs and shrimp that writhed about on the display table, although I sometimes ate them at other people's homes. I never did learn to eat freshly sliced garlic cloves, which were quite popular with the Chinese, beginning with breakfast, and whose vapors were not easily disguised by toothpaste and/or mouthwash. I did learn to like persimmon, deviled quail eggs, moon cakes, duck, and the ever-popular steamed dumplings (joudza).

Restaurants and Eating Out

Kan da gee (Kahn da gee) KFC; Macadona's (maca donna's) McDonalds

For our first few months in China, eating out was only done with other people, No one in the restaurants spoke English. We were the only westerners (Lao ai -foreign devils) in our area of town. We were never quite sure how welcome we really were. In fact, one time a taxi driver spent the duration of our ride yelling George Bush – buo hao, buo hao at me. I was terrified he was going to murder me and dump me in some terrible place.

We did, however, go to dinner with friends. As we became more familiar with the city, we discovered there were western style restaurants on the other side of town. They served more familiar foods and spoke English. We went to the Lido hotel for its wonderful French restaurant and bakery. We went to Gua Mao world trade center for pizza. We went to the Friendship hotel for Friday's restaurant. And over by Lufthansa center there was an Outback Steak House. We also discovered the Lufthansa Center had a wonderful Sunday buffet and we went there a few times.

And we discovered that Beijing had a "Macadona's", Pizza Hut, and Kan da gee (KFC). No one spoke English, but we could use our fledgling Chinese and point. No Taco Bell, though. I was told it was because the Chinese tended to be lactose intolerant, although that didn't seem to fit with having Pizza Hut. We never went to Chinese restaurants on our own, as we were skittish about what we might be served with our poor command of the language. I knew how to say green beans – gan bian si ji dou – and ice cream -bing qi ling, but that was pretty limiting.

There were plenty of street venders, as well. Some were cooking enormous omelet-like offerings that looked delicious. The cook would heat up a giant handled griddle. He would pour an egg-batter on it and swish it around like a crepe. As it cooked, he would add a wide variety of vegetables, roll it up and wrap it in paper. It was not recommended by our contacts to eat these, so we passed. But they looked and smelled wonderful. We did purchase roasted chestnuts and sweet potatoes, though, and thoroughly enjoyed them.

Pizza Hut was a great place to people-watch. Young Beijingers loved it. It had a salad bar. But the rule was you only got one trip to the bar. And the bowls were small. It was funny to watch the diners fill their bowl to the brim, then build a wall of crackers around the sides of the bowl and fill it to at least twice its height. They definitely got their money's worth. It just goes to show people everywhere want a bargain and will try to outwit the system.

Phones – Phone Books, Finding Numbers

Wei? (way) Hello (This is a typical greeting when answering the phone)

We went to Beijing just as cell phones were becoming popularized. As Head of School, I was provided with a red flip phone. I didn't know one could program frequently dialed numbers into it. Actually, I don't think I knew any numbers! Later, when I did, I carried them around with me on a piece of paper in my wallet, but few people had cell phones, so I didn't make a lot of calls. And I didn't attend it when it rang. More than once, my fiscal officer called my secretary to have her tell me to answer my phone!

On one particular occasion, I was on my way home from a school function. The taxi driver's phone kept ringing and ringing. I couldn't imagine why he didn't answer it. It would ring, ring, ring, and then stop; ring, ring, ring, and then stop. It was becoming a little annoying. Suddenly, on the fourth iteration the taxi driver turned to me and said in an irritated and perfect English, "Answer your phone".

Calls to the United States were pricey. We soon learned that we could purchase phone cards for very cheap on the Black Market, in an area that was close to the Antique Market. Our Board contact took us there once and helped us purchase cards. After that, we were on our own to rediscover the place and purchase what we needed.

The cards worked well. The process was just to pick up the land line phone and type in the 10-digit number on the card. Then you could input the number you were calling and you would be connected. Unfortunately, the system did not warn you when your minutes were almost up, so you had to watch the clock. Sometimes, though, you just got cut off because the system was imprecise. Anyway, we were able to call home and did so weekly, which took the edge off homesickness.

Learning Chinese – The Relentless Star

Ti gueila! (Tie guay la!) It's too expensive!;
Qing gui (ching guay) Light rail; Fa piao (fa
piow) ticket

It might surprise the Chinese to hear this, but the Chinese language, maybe because of cadence or delivery of the speaker, always sounds sharp and harsh, even angry. At first it seemed like whenever I heard people talking, they were agitated and upset with one another. I still recall a woman in an open market approaching us and "yao ma?" She was only saying "what do you want/how can I help you," but for all I knew she was yelling "get out here, you devil!" It might have helped if she had smiled, but that was not the case. Serious faces and barked statements did not register as welcoming. We were not China-phyles. We spoke no Chinese. We knew nothing about Chinese customs or culture. China wasn't even on our list of American-friendly countries. And yet there we were.

My staff was always helpful. For a while, I ate lunch with the staff in the break room. Everyone was helpful, especially the Chinese staff who seemed to enjoy providing me with mini lessons in Chinese words and phrases about eating. It wasn't long before I could identify foods and utensils by their Chinese names – tudo for potato; Wo chi, I am eating/ate, I'm hungry, Wo yao for I want, etc. I had bought a little language book (doesn't everyone?) to start the process of learning common words and phrases, which at least gave people the impression that we knew something. The unintended consequence of using a phrase, of course, was that the person you spoke to assumed you spoke Chinese and responded with lots of dialogue you couldn't understand. When we knew we had to go somewhere or buy a specific item, my secretary would write the information down in Chinese, so I could show the note to the taxi driver or shop keeper. That usually worked, but it eliminated doing or needing anything on the spur of the moment.

We needed a tutor. As it happened, in August, our primary school CSL (Chinese as a Second Language) teacher moved away. Or maybe she retired. Or she could have had a beef with other teachers. I wasn't exactly sure. There was a lot of conversation, and the Head of School Emeritus was translating in short bursts, so I knew I wasn't getting all the details. Anyway, she was gone. We had to find a new teacher. Our general manager was able to hire a local Chinese woman who had a young child and whose husband was studying at a nearby university. She called herself Star. She was wonderful with the children. She was always kind and smiling. She rotated from elementary classroom to classroom teaching both oral and written Chinese to children from 5 to 10 years old.

We approached her to see if she would be our tutor. She agreed to meet with us one day a week to help us learn Chinese. I was a committed student. I had my notebook. I practiced. I listened, I wrote. I repeated. I responded. My husband dragged his feet. He didn't hear the tones, He didn't remember the words. His heart just wasn't in it. He was already experiencing culture shock and was pretty miserable. He did like Star, though. So, for her, he made an effort. Sometimes Star took us on field trips, so we could learn the words while we were involved in the activity. One day she took us to Hong Chow market (the Pearl Market). It's probably the best-known market in Beijing for tourists. It's always packed with them. We learned to bargain in Chinese – Tai gueila! Too much!

One day we met at the school and walked to the Light Rail Station. During the entire walk, Star spoke to us in Chinese, elicited our responses, pointed to items and had us practice new vocabulary, quizzed us, corrected us. She was relentless. She never let up. She never let us off the hook. We went to the ticket booth and purchased a ticket – fa piao. We boarded the light rail – chin guay. We road all the way to the downtown – no English, only Chinese. On the way back, my head hurt from trying so hard. My brain rebelled. "No, Star, I said. "I can't do any more. My brain hurts. I just need to be quiet". Star laughed and agreed to ease up. By the time we were walking back to the school, however, she had started up again, and I was rested up enough to comply with her instructions and questions. She was an outstanding teacher – Star, the relentless!

Even after we left China, we continued to have a relationship with Star. She had become a close and trusted friend. We had met her daughter, Lucy, and her husband and occasionally went to dinner with them. We were able to communicate via email. In 2010 when we made a return trip, we were able to connect with her. Her husband had finished school and her daughter was planning to attend university in the United States.

As the time for her daughter to come to the states drew near, Star emailed us she would be coming with her. We planned to travel to the college to meet them and have a reunion. Star said she would contact us as soon as they arrived. Then everything went dark. The communication never came. The email sent to her was returned as undeliverable. I tried through mutual friends to locate her, to locate her daughter, but every effort just led to a dead end. Sadly, we have never heard from Star again. She was a special friend. I always hoped she would be able to visit us in the United States someday, but I suppose that won't happen.

Using the Postal Service

Youjian (Yo gee ann) Mail

Nothing in China was easy. Everything was convoluted, with twists and turns and restarts. Many things were intimidating and nerve wracking. There were mailboxes in the entryway of our apartment. We had a key. We received mail. We were also able to mail letters with school mail which was dropped off by someone each day. We did not receive packages, however. A notification of a package meant a trip downtown with Star. Packages had already been opened and searched before we received them. You had to prove your identity and pay a fee for their release.

When SARs hit, we were in need of masks and thermometers for our school and our families. I reached out to my Rotary in the USA to ask for donations. When the package came, it was rerouted to the mayor of the Haidian district. We were informed the package would cost $700 in tariffs to retrieve. Our Business Manager told me if we gave the mayor half of the items in the package, we would not have to pay. I couldn't believe we were being extorted! Back and forth the conversation went. When we were done, the mayor took 25 percent of the items meant for our school and our families. Urghhh!

Sending packages was another game entirely. When we started packing to return to the United States, we learned we had to take our items to a special post office. The items were not to be boxed or sealed. On a morning, we filled our two largest suitcases with all the items we wanted to ship home. We walked to the taxi stand and loaded them up. The taxi took us to a rather ominous/official building. In a cramped and poorly lit room the workers went through our suitcases, searching, looking at everything.

Then they sold us boxes we had to use to pack the items. We brought our own packing materials – tape, mailing labels, markers, and bubble wrap - as they were not available at the mailing place. There was one small table in the room. There was nowhere to sit. We opted to work on the floor. We packed up each of our boxes and crouched over them one at a time to fill out a form that itemized exactly what was in the box. Then we went back to the window. The workers went through the box and checked everything again. Then they signed the voucher. Finally, we were allowed to seal our packages and address them. We paid and were given copies of our vouchers. We worried our boxes would never make it back to the US, but when we arrived, they were there waiting for us.

Standing in Line

The Chinese do not stand in line. They crowd in line. We learned this when we went to Ikea to return something. We went to customer service. We took a spot we thought was the end of the line. After a dozen people had walked in and moved right in front of us, crowding up to the counter, we took the hint. Bill muscled us up to the front and we took care of our business. We saw the same behavior wherever we went. He that can muscle to the front goes first. Bill became quite good at it!

We also saw the same behavior manifest itself on the street. Enormous traffic jams were created when every driver crowded up and maneuvered for every inch of space, refusing to give any advantage to other drivers. Eventually the authorities would come and sort it out, unraveling car after car from the jumble and sending them on their way.

My own driver was an expert at making his own lane. It was not uncommon for him when we were in a traffic jam to swing into the bike lane, or even onto the other side of the street to get ahead. After a few weeks of sheer un-seat-belted terror, I resigned myself to going with the flow. And not once did we hit anything or anyone!

Red Light, Green Light

Yoguai (Yo gwhy) to the right; Zhoguai (Zo gwhy) to the left; Y ji zo (Y jur zo) Straight ahead

I am sitting in the back seat of a taxi. No seat belt. Hot. Late for a meeting. We are in a traffic jam. The lanes are packed on our right. The bike lane next to that is bustling. The frontage road is filled with donkey carts, wagons, bikes and pedestrians. Red light.

Across the median, there is no oncoming traffic. My driver suddenly yanks the steering wheel to the left and slams on the accelerator. The car leaps across the median and we race along on the wrong side of the road. Two intersections later, he jerks the vehicle right and we are at the front of the line waiting at another red light. I am unfazed, dozing. This is the norm. On another day we might swing into the bike or frontage lanes. Or run the red light altogether.

We did not purchase a vehicle while we were in Beijing. We couldn't read road signs, the traffic was terrifying, and we didn't know the driving rules. We walked, took a taxi, or accessed by driver. We could have gotten bicycles but didn't. Again, the traffic. We marveled at the bikes whizzing around without getting creamed by freewheeling cars. Taxis were not difficult to access from our complex at most any time. They were also available throughout the city when businesses were open. Although the city was relatively safe, we didn't go out frequently at night as we didn't really know our way around.

My husband and I never figured out the red light – green light system. Sometimes we would come to a red light and drive right through it. Sometimes the driver stopped. We postulated that at intersections where there was a traffic cop or a traffic camera, people stopped for the red light. If those two deterrents were not in place, the rules were out the window.

Lane lines also seemed to only be suggestions. 3-lane boulevards were often made into 5 lanes by the Chinese drivers. Chinese were not good about standing in line and waiting for their turn. On the roads, just like in the stores, they pushed and crowded to get to the front. Traffic jams were most often created by everyone trying to be in the same place at once.

The Beijing city road infrastructure was a highway that was intersected by 5 concentric, circular roads, modeled after a bull's eye. The downtown area was at the center, like a hub. Each "ring road" or beltway, circled the hub in ever expanding circles, The first ring road was at the hub. We lived off of the third ring road San Huan Lu, on Xi San Chi. We lived in the Fang Dan Li Shu apartments (Fountainbleu). Taxis liked to transport us back and forth from there because it was a long way from everything, so it was a good fare. There was also a light rail that circled the city, and my husband rode it to the first ring road and the Canadian Embassy.

My husband learned and practiced how to give directions to a Chinese cabbie. Yo guay - left, Zo guay - right, Y ji zo – straight ahead. I believe it gave him some sense of control in a world that was continuously confounding.

We also found it intriguing that at dusk, and even into night, many Chinese did not turn on their lights. As you were driving along, vehicles would wizz by you that you didn't even realize were there. We never did figure out for what purpose they were saving their lights. Maybe batteries didn't last long or were easily depleted. I suspect it was really because cars were a relatively new addition to Chinese life and people just didn't know the safety importance of turning on the lights of the car. Now that we are back in the states, we fondly bestow the name "China driver" to Americans who drive without turning on their headlights.

Shopping

Shao Bai Yan (Shaow by yawn) The Little
White Goat Grocery Store; Wo yao (Wah yow)
I want; Woju (wah dju) Lettuce

I like to shop. I like to window shop. I have shopped in other countries, so I know my way around a local market. I love the game of bargaining. Once in Playa del Carmen a shopkeeper told me, "You are the cheapest lady I have ever seen!" All in good fun. At least he called me a lady!

Shopping in China was challenging. It didn't take me long to realize this was the immigrant experience – not understanding the language, not being able to read the labels, the money, and what was nestled behind the packaging. Wo yao was only useful if you could then say what it was you wanted. I learned the words for chicken, pork, beef, etc. after a time, but not being able to read the mandarin on labels had some funny results.

I purchased a quart of what I thought was milk. It was yogurt. I bought a package of pot roast. It smelled and tasted different – although it was edible. We were told later it was either donkey or horse. We bought what looked like steak and Bill grilled it. It was pretty good. When I was explaining to one of my Chinese teachers what we ate, she said, "Oh, yes! Eyebrow meat." That was a big "Oh, no!" for me. The first food word we learned in China was bing qi ling – ice cream. We bought some, which identified a second challenge for us. We were used to big refrigerators and ample freezers. We had a hobbit-sized refrigerator. Chinese people shopped every day. We wanted to shop every week, like we did in the States.

Varieties of bread were not the staple in China. We were able to buy a small cube-shaped loaf at Shao Bai Yan. So we would try to buy three every week so we could have toast and sandwiches. We had a freezer that didn't hold much, so it was always crammed full. Fresh vegetables and fruits were easier, because we could recognize them. Canned and packaged items were difficult.

We bought tuna. The cans looked similar to those in the US. It took three tries to get regular tuna fish, however. Once we came home with tuna and red bean paste, once with something unrecognizable and inedible.

We were so hungry for western bread at the time, we decided to try to make bagels, so we needed flour. At the store, we had to decide whether to buy the package of flour with the red printing or the flour with the green printing. We picked the green and got regular flour. The red, we learned later, was self-rising. But who would know?

The bagels were great, and I made them for a while, until Bill discovered Jenny Lu's, just a block from the Canadian Embassy. Jenny Lu's was a western grocery store, and they had bagels. We didn't go there often, because it was an hour away from our home and much more expensive than local markets, but we did go.

Iceberg lettuce was another item not in demand in the area we lived (there were very few foreign devils – Laowai – so there wasn't a lot of call for it). One day I found three tiny heads, which I joyfully grabbed up. The greengrocer grunted at me happily and I grunted back. He said a word I didn't recognize and couldn't say well - woju. "Lettuce," I said. He butchered the English, and told me the word in Chinese again. I butchered the Chinese! We both laughed and bowed.

We were ecstatic! The lettuce was so delicious, with tomatoes, cukes in oil and vinegar! The next week, when the greengrocer saw me, he excitedly motioned me to the stand where he had placed three heads. "Ledas," he said. Woju. "Hao, lettuce," I answered in English and tried to mimic the Chinese word. He laughed and shook his head. Of course, I bought them all, and from then on, he always had lettuce for me. He was a very astute businessman, catering to the needs of his clientele. And I was hooked. I was a regular.

Sometimes I wonder whether he looked for me when we left China. Did he wonder what happened to me that I no longer came to his stand? I still think of him sometimes and his kind and smiling face. He was such a pleasant highlight of my shopping experience. It's amazing, isn't it, how such a simple thing as a smile or a saved head of lettuce can affect our entire day.

Finding Western Foods

Poersumata (Poe air suh ma ta) Price Mart.

We went grocery shopping on Saturday or Sunday mornings, depending on whether we had tourist or school activities going on. By the end of the first summer, we had discovered Po er su mata and Jenny Lu. Po er su mata (Pricemart) was a box store and it was a very new and exciting thing in Beijing. It was about an hour's taxi drive from our apartment complex. At 8:00 a.m., we would walk down the Champs Elysses to the gate of the complex and find a taxi. Some days it was difficult to make ourselves understood, so I always carried a note my secretary, Tina, had written – "Please take us to Pricemart." We would speed down the beltways, streets and avenues, looking at signs written in Chinese characters undecipherable to the untrained eye.

It was at Pricemart we discovered our mini oven. And in a far back corner of the store, we discovered another windfall. A western food section. Hormel, Cheerios, Contadina, Nabisco, and more. The section was not large, and the items were expensive, but it was comforting to buy a familiar this and that. For our turkey-less Thanksgiving, I found a can of OceanSpray cranberry sauce.

The meat counter in grocery stores was very similar to what we knew from the United States. Many items – chicken, pork chops, beef, whole duck were usually easy enough to identify.

I learned later that beef was not as easy as I thought. One day I came home with horse or donkey pot roast instead of beef. It didn't taste bad, but we knew right away it wasn't beef.

Buying seafood was not an experience for the faint of heart. Piles of live shrimp and crab crawled over one another on a 6 x 6 table. You told the vendor what you wanted and he packaged it for you. The creatures were crawling and pulling all over each other and often fell to the floor to be scooped back up by the vendor. The smell can only be described as ripe. Fish, on the other hand, were in a tank. You picked the fish you wanted and the vendor caught it, dispatched it and wrapped it up. We had seafood a few times while we were in China, thanks to friends and restaurants who knew how to deal with it, but I never bought it from the market. And I didn't buy the shrimp or crab either.

Jenny Lu's was also an hour away from our home, but it was like a trip to Disneyland. Although it was the size of an old corner market in the states, all the foods were western, with the exception of the produce. Everything was recognizable. They had such delicacies as bagels. They had Hormel hams and bacon. The labels were in English. The salespeople spoke English.

There was a downside to Jenny Lu's, however. It was far from anything. Chinese people didn't shop there. Westerners who shopped there lived in the area and drove their own cars. Taxis were uncommon. Often, we would sit outside on the bench for over half an hour before a taxi might pass by. Pricemart, on the other hand was always crowded with Chinese customers who were intrigued by the box store experience, and taxis abounded.

After shopping, we would hail a taxi and spend another hour going home. We would collect our groceries out of the trunk (often with the help of our doorman). We unbagged and put everything away. I filled the sink with water from the 5-gallon bottle and washed the vegetables and fruit, leaving it to air dry on the counter.

Fruits and vegetables were abundant and delicious. We bought yard long green beans and garlic stalks. We bought persimmons and pomelos. Bread products were limited, but we bought small 6-inch cubes of sliced yeast bread when we found them. They were similar to a package of store-brand sliced sandwich bread, but about a fourth of the length, so they looked like a cube. They were actually quite good, and we could even toast them in our tiny toaster oven.

The Russian Market

Tai guai la. (Tie quay la) It's too expensive

Shopping in Beijing was always an adventure. There were many small shops and markets. When we were looking for walking shoes for Bill and winter jackets for each of us, we were referred to the Russian Market. It think it was called Ya Bao Lu and it was an hour's drive from where we lived. We had only been in the city for a couple of months and were still struggling with the language. I had a cell phone, but the only numbers I knew were on my desk in my office. So going somewhere we were unfamiliar with was a little scary. Anyway, my secretary wrote notes for me to give taxis so we could get there and get home.

The Russian Market was enormous – three huge Quonset hut affairs that covered three city blocks. Inside were endless rows of booths selling everything from clothing to household items. There was really nothing Russian about it, but because it sold a lot of "western" clothing, the Chinese dubbed it so. No one spoke much English, although one young lady taught me to say "tai guai la" (too much).

On our first visit, we walked up and down the rows together looking for and purchasing small items. We found a booth that had winter jackets and tried them on. I stepped out to the next booth, but finding nothing of interest, went back to the jacket booth. Bill was not there. I backed out into the corridor and looked in the nearby booths. I called out his name. We were close to the back entrances and I heard a hubbub there that included raised voices and what sounded like a struggle. I called out to Bill again. I could not locate my husband. I waited for several minutes, which felt more loke several years. I walked around and came back to the jacket booth. Then I walked to the front entrance, thinking he might have gone there looking for me. After waiting for a few minutes, I retraced my steps to the jacket booth. Nobody. I called out again. Nothing. There I was in an unfamiliar place, no one who could understand me, no one I could call.

I was suddenly frightened. And I was starting to panic. I had visions of my husband being kidnapped; dragged out the rear door of the market to be murdered or held for ransom. I walked to the end of the row and called out for Bill one more time, and heard a rather muffled "What?" I followed the sound and there he was in the next row. I was ecstatic! He was totally unaware that we had become separated or that I was afraid for his safety. The tears on my face spoke volumes. We finished our shopping trip, found a taxi and gave the driver directions to take us home. I later came to know that my fears about kidnapping and murder were largely unfounded. Just the result of reading and watching too many mystery stories. Despite its size, Beijing was a very safe place, and the authorities did not tolerate any ill treatment of westerners. Good to know.

We went back to the Russian market several times, and then on another trip found it gone. As if it had never existed. There was just a big hole in the ground. And no one we knew had any idea what had happened to it or if it had moved to another venue. We asked and we got answers like "maybe it moved to a different area", and "maybe they will rebuild it somewhere else." As I have gone back to review my communications with our Chinese acquaintances, I have become convinced that "maybe" meant something else like "I think." Anyway, we were never able to locate the market again. When we returned to China several years later, we discovered Ya Bao Lu was in full operation near the Beijing Children's Hospital and Ritan Park.

Additional Markets

The Flower Market.

Every Chinese grocery store and outdoor market contained a flower market. Even the outdoor areas had an enclosure filled with blooms. At first, I ignored these, knowing how expensive bouquets in the states were. I mentioned the flowers to my secretary, Julia, and she said they were very inexpensive. The next time I went to Shao Bai Yan, I purchased an exquisite bouquet of yellow roses and baby's breath for $3.00, and I was hooked. We had fresh flowers in our apartment every week from then on. They cheered the place and gave me a frivolous outlet.

The Antique Market – Panjaoyuan oldah old

Like so many Western tourists, we were interested in purchasing souvenirs and treasures to take back to the states. The antique market, therefore, was a place we visited. It was filled with vendors selling "oldah" items to tourists willing to believe they were buying an antique. Once an item was sold and the buyer had moved on, the seller took an identical item out of his pack and displayed it for the next client. We found nothing of any great interest in Panjaoyuan, but there was an open air food market just down the road, so we went there to see what it was about.

The Open-Air Market

One of the most interesting components of the open-air market was it had a section of vendors that were dealing in nuts – all kinds of them. We stopped at the booth of a middle-aged woman with long, wild hair and flowing clothing who looked to be Mongolian. Her English was as poor as my Chinese, but we had a wonderful time dickering over the prices of almonds, walnuts, cashews, pecans, hazelnuts, and chestnuts. She patiently taught me the name of each, tried to help me understand pricing, and was delighted to have me inquire and purchase in Chinese. All that year, our coffee table had bowls and baskets filled with nuts, always many more than we needed, just so we could go back to see our nut seller. Then one day we went to the market and she was gone. She wasn't there the next week either. When I explained the issue to my school secretary, she shrugged and said she probably went home to Mongolia. I was crushed (no pun intended)! And once again, I experienced a situation far from any control I might exert.

When the world rushes by you in an unfamiliar cadence, it is easy to become disoriented and discouraged. As an immigrant, you really never know for sure what is going on. You are dependent on the kindness of others. You keep to yourself rather than getting into an awkward or dangerous situation. Although, I have to say there was not a lot of danger in Beijing. Petty crime was practically nonexistent, and criminals were dealt with harshly by the government.

Hong Ciao Market (Hong Chow)

The Pearl Market - Hong Ciao - was the ultimate tourist market in Bejing. All tourists were routed there. It had several stories of booths and shops and offered anything from jewelry (especially pearls) to food. The Board wives took me there when they were courting me. I went back on occasion to purchase gifts (again pearls). It was always fun to get into the mix of bartering/ bargaining.

I recall shopping for some Christmas gifts and I wanted to get cashmere scarves for all the ladies in my family. There was a little booth that had a wide variety of scarves and shawls. I had picked out 9 scarves I liked. The shopkeeper stated her price. I countered a low-ball offer. The shopkeeper reacted with fake dismay and alarm (as expected) and shot out a price a bit lower than her original. I laughed and again offered a very low amount. The shopkeeper reacted with sharp words and flailing arms. She dropped the price a smidge. I came back with the same amount as my last offer; stated I was, after all, buying 9. She yelled at me and tore the scarves from my arms and threw them into her stall. Surprised, my husband and I turned and started on to the next stand. Someone grabbed my sleeve from behind. "Ok, ok," said the scarf shopkeeper, shoving a bag of scarves in my arms. I paid for the merchandise (at my price) and moved on. It was a great shopping day. I got what I was willing to pay and the shopkeeper made a profit, because the items were greatly overpriced.

CHAPTER 4

On Being a Tourist

*Laowai (lao why) Foreign Devil; Meguoran
(May guo ron) American*

WE DIDN'T HAVE A CAR WHILE WE WERE IN CHINA. AS I THINK ABOUT it, I don't believe any of our teaching staff did either. Everyone took the bus, the chingway, the taxi, or biked and walked. The school's Business Director made sure we all had opportunities to visit the main tourist sites. Bill and I were connected with a Chinese couple who took us to the Peiking Man site and the Temple of the Moon. He also arranged group trips to the Great Wall, to a temple/restaurant to celebrate Chinese New Year, and to the Ming tombs. We took taxis to Tienamen Square and the Palace and to the Pearl and Antique markets. I also had a driver and I was able to arrange for him to take us to places of interest, as well. Because our apartment complex was in a newer, undeveloped area far removed from central hubs, we didn't do much walking.

Peiking Man Site

We were impressed by the Peiking Man site, which had been well preserved by the Chinese government and the site and museum were interesting. Unfortunately, many of the artifacts were stolen by the Japanese when they overran the country and have never been returned, so there were gaps. The area was wooded and cool, which meant a lot since Beijing summers were hot and muggy.

Tienamen Square

Tienamen was imposing and austere. It felt unapproachable. As many times as we passed it during our time in Beijing, there was a dearth of people, in glaring contrast to the protests and massacre that took place there in June of 1989. It was hard to imagine up to one million demonstrators, many of them students, packing the square, demanding more political freedom. The government sent in the army to crush the protests, and it is estimated that over 200 students were killed and another 3,000 were injured. We discovered quickly that the Chinese were not kindly disposed to talk about it, but it was unclear whether that was out of fear or embarrassment. Anyway, we passed by the Square regularly, and it was always deserted.

The Great Wall of China Chang cheng (Chang Cheng) The Long Wall

When we think of China, something that almost always comes to mind is the Great Wall. It winds for about 13,100 miles from east to west across the northern regions, sometimes in sections, sometimes doubling up on itself. When I made my first trip to Beijing for interviews, I was treated to a tour of the Wall at the Badaling site, a well-restored section that is popular for tourists. It was impressive. But throughout our time in China, we visited other, unrestored sections, scrambling up the side to tumbled watchtowers and walking along the crumbling cobblestones of the 500-year-old structure. I have to say it was like walking through the old parts of many European cities. History seems to swirl around you, and the voices of the past murmur on the wind.

The Great Wall was, indeed, great! We visited it at Ba Da Ling, a tourist location that had been beautifully restored, and included a museum and lots of shops. At that location, one sees it in what must have been its glory, towering to heights of at least 3 times the height of a man. We also visited the 500-year-old fortification at two other places that had not been restored. Negotiating the 15-foot-wide, now crumbling track, it was easy to imagine soldiers marching or riding their horses along its many miles. We were told, however, that many sections of the wall were only wide enough for one person, and mounted soldiers had to ride along its base. Sadly, the old adage that it was the only feature on the earth that could be seen from the moon, was disproved by the astronauts.

Ming Tombs

I can't say much about the Ming Tombs, because they were in the middle of the "jungle", and were not restored, so we could only walk so close to them. Grasses and bushes had overgrown the entire area. It was quite remote, eerily quiet, and, although I'm sure there was nothing dangerous lurking in the brush, we were fine with distance observing. If I were to go to China again, I would take tour buses to all the venues. I think it's worth the cost to have guides with the knowledge to educate you on what you are seeing.

Xi'an

We planned to take the train to Xi'an to see the terracotta warriors in the spring, but never made it. As SARs became more concerning, people were restricted by the government from traveling. Then there was no travel at all allowed for a period of time.

Reflections

Bill and I were both "well traveled" when we went to China, but the experience was eye-opening for me for realizing the depths of my ignorance about the world. There is so much to know, and we merely know a drop of it. We develop pre-conceived ideas about peoples, cultures, that are excruciatingly shallow. The opportunity to travel provides opportunities to deepen one's understanding of others if you open yourself to it.

Unfortunately, it can also reinforce a person's biases. For example, I am an optimistic and enthusiastic gardener. We had a big yard. I could have planted flowers or vegetables, but I never touched the soil. It sounds crazy, but it felt totally alien to me, and I believe I had a vague, unformed fear of what Chinese soil contained. I never articulated it while in the country, but I have reflected on it since our return. I don't know if I would have felt that on Spanish, Italian or German soil. Unconscious bias is hard to identify, so hard to change. Our hidden biases interfere with openness to one another unless we can root them out and inspect them.

Chinese Resorts

Yule (you lay) recreation; Wan de kaixin (Juan du kai shin) Have fun!

On one occasion, we took the teachers on an excursion to a resort preferred by the local population. The buildings were rustic, made of some kind of stucco. Each cabin had a 5x6 foot raised stage on one side. The stage area was about 18 inches above the floor and was hollow. On its side was a wooden door that opened into the hollow space. The stage was actually a bed. Mats and blankets were placed on the stage for the patron's comfort. An attendant would build a fire earlier in the day in the hollow area under the bed. When the fire had burned itself out, the stage walls and floor were warm and ready for the night. What a clever idea! It gave new meaning to putting something under the bed!

The resort had other features. There were two large manmade ponds that were filled with fish. We were invited to "go fishing" in the ponds. Several teachers and their children caught fish. We handed the catch over to an attendant. When a picnic lunch was served, our recently caught fish were a part of the menu, served whole. Our Chinese hosts jockeyed for the eyes, which were a highly prized delicacy! Non-Chinese staff and their families hung back from sampling.

In the late spring we went on an excursion to another resort to go hiking, again along the Great Wall. When we returned from our mountain/wall trek, we were provided with lunch. This time stewed chicken, a kind of hard corn bread, and vegetables. When the head and feet of the chickens appeared in the pot, I thought my poor husband was going to have a heart attack. He was as hungry as the rest of us, but he ate nothing. My thinking was as long as I didn't have to have those items on my plate, everything was "mei guanchi" – no problem.

CHAPTER 5

School Is School Isn't True

Preparing for Fall Semester: Xin Shi Fu, Cheung Laoshi and the Team

> *Xuexiao (shoo eh shaow) school; Xuesheng (shoo eh shawng) student*

INTERNATIONAL SCHOOLS IN BEIJING CATER TO A WIDE VARIETY OF students from many countries. During the summers, expats from all over the globe move into the city with their families and investigate what schools have to offer. The International School of Beijing and the Western Academy of Beijing were the largest schools. Some of the embassies had small schools, but those were typically only for the children of embassy employees. There were additional smaller schools like ours, NSCL, the New School of Collaborative Learning.

As soon as I began working at NSCL in the summer of 2002, the Finance Director informed me we were moving. He had found a better, newer building, located on a college campus, which had more modern facilities and extensive grounds for physical education activities. The facility just needed some renovation. He took me to the building to secure my approval in order for the lease to be signed and the renovation to begin. The Board was in favor of the move. I gave the ok.

Maybe I was just hot and miserable from the weather and discouraged by what I'd seen, but I told my husband that night that I thought the "new" building was going to need a lot more than a little renovation. Yes, it was less than 5-years-old, but the white exterior walls were already encrusted with the grimy air of the city and were the color of the gray air around them. The treads on the stairs were worn away up the middle. The fetid odor of the restrooms permeated everything on the three stories we were to occupy. Windows were broken, walls were gray. It looked like it had been built 50 years ago. And did I mention the restrooms? Absolutely horrible! But the Finance Director laughed good naturedly and said it would all be up to snuff by the start of school.

Now Beijing in the summer is hot and muggy. From the moment you step out your front door, you are damp. Your clothes are sticky, your hair becomes curly and unruly. Your makeup wears away as you wipe the perspiration off your face for the hundredth time. You feel like you are melting. If your school building is being repurposed, there are days without air conditioning. If you are moving, everyone is packing and there are boxes and debris everywhere. Much of the furniture is gone. The walls are bare.

Picture that welcoming atmosphere as your secretary steps into your office (at this time just a closet with a desk and a chair), to tell you the Egyptian Consul and his wife are here to see you about enrolling their children in the school. Yikes! We met in the main office. We sat on chairs that were marked for disposal, the metal was rusting, the cerulean upholstery torn and faded. The air conditioning had been out all morning. The Consul was wearing a tan suit. His wife was in green and gold chintz with a wrap (I thought she must have been sweltering!) and an exotic gold necklace and earring combination. I apologized for the disarray and explained about the new facility we were moving into. We talked about the advantages of going to the school, about extra-curricular activities, about tuition. They took a brochure and my card. Their children were not among the enrollees when we opened the new school in the fall. Sad, but not surprising.

Mr. Xin

Xin shi fu (shin sure foo) Master Xin

Our head custodian was Mr. Xin - Xin Shu Fu. Shu Fu is a title of respect meaning "master". So, he was Master Xin. And he was. If it was broken, Mr. Xin could fix it. He was a slight man with a very pleasant, wrinkled face and ready smile. When I first met him, I believed him to be in his seventies. To describe him physically I would use words like stooped, wizened, wrinkled. He was also agile, quick, strong, perceptive, and clever. He commanded a cadre of Ai's, who cleaned the building and the buses, and a company of bus drivers who took children to and from school and transported them on field trips. They also carried staff to entertainment activities that were arranged at least monthly – picnics, resorts stays, the opera, tourist attractions, to name a few.

Mr. Xin spoke no English. My Chinese was little more than grunts. Nevertheless, he sought me out to show me what needed to be taken care of or repaired or what he had done. He lived in a small room at the back of the copy room and went to visit his family on the weekends. On occasion, he would come into my office before school and sit down in front of my desk. He would unpack a pair of hot sweet potatoes and give one to me. On the white paper napkins I provided, we would peel our potatoes and eat them. "Nangua," he would say. "Hao." "Hun hao," I would reply, savoring the hot, sweet flesh. I was later taught the word for potato was "tudo" and nangua was pumpkin. However, we never saw a pumpkin in China, so I think nangua was the word for sweet potato.

Xin was not what he appeared to be on the surface. He was much younger than he looked. With his deeply wrinkled hands and face, white hair, his limp, his stooped appearance, I would have guessed him to be 70. Xin was nearer my age than 70. He had been detained and tortured during the Mao regime for using a board with a picture of Mao on it to repair a hole in his wall. He was accused of subversion. Then, for whatever reason, after a period of time in prison, he was released. He went home, but his health was impaired, he limped, he was stooped his hair had turned white. He took up smoking, a terrible habit enjoyed by so many Chinese. That, and the poor air quality in Beijing, resulted in him having a terrible, rasping cough.

Xin didn't just take care of the school. He often helped the teachers with problems they had at their apartments. Teacher's apartments were leased by the school and were thus as extension of the building. Xin was a carpenter, plumber and electrician all rolled into one. He did not have state-of-the-art tools; his were older, bulkier, more cumbersome. But he made them work. My husband and I missed having an oven, since Chinese kitchens are not equipped with them. At the box store, Poer si ma tah, we encountered and purchased a toaster oven. Imagine the smallest microwave you have ever seen. That was our oven. We couldn't find any cooking vessels that were small enough to fit inside. Finally, at the department store next to Shao Bai Yan, I found a small blue casserole dish. It was a perfect fit. It yielded exactly two helpings of whatever food I baked. We flew to the states for Christmas that year, and I found a tiny metal cookie sheet from a children's Take and Bake oven. When we got back to China, Xin cut it to a size that would fit into our tiny oven (and made sure it was smoothed and rounded so it would not cut anyone). It was a major obstacle overcome! I could bake cookies – 4 at a time!

Several years after we left Beijing, I learned the school had closed. I always wondered if Xin went back to the countryside.

School Staff

Laoshi (laow sure) teacher

International schools get a fascinating mix of teaching staff. Most come for the adventure of being able to live and travel in another country and building their resume. Some come for the financial benefits. Some are enamored of the country itself. For all, it is part of a journey.

Our school certainly had its share of noteworthy personalities. For example, the school had an American second grade teacher whose husband was completing his doctorate at a Bei Da, the main university. They and their two children spoke fluent Chinese and embraced the culture passionately. She took me shopping early on to a local "department store" that was actually more of a flea market. No one spoke any English, so I stuck close to watch the customer/vendor back and forth. I learned some language that helped me greatly later on when my husband and I ventured into markets on our own. Yao ma? What do you want. Wo yao. I want. Tai gueila. Too much.

Our school was unique in that we were a bilingual environment. The children were from many countries, although we were not allowed to enroll Chinese children. We were an English-speaking school, but we also taught the children to speak Chinese since they were living in China. In that vein, for each classroom we had the regular English-speaking teacher and a

Chinese team-teacher. (As you might imagine, teacher-student ratio was great!)

One second grade team teacher was Cheung Laoshi. – In my mind I called her Lady C. She was very prim and proper and always had a very carefully articulated response to share her concern that things or people did not suit her. When observing that classroom, I noticed the American teacher took great pains to demonstrate respect for her. Their relationship was painfully formal. Lady C's husband was an artist. When we moved into our new school, I thought it would benefit the school and the local art community if we displayed local artwork. After some negotiation, Lady C's husband kindly loaned us artwork to decorate the walls of our new school building. It was stunning! I still have the lovely floral piece that hung in my office. When I left the school, my staff purchased the painting and gave it to me as a remembrance. Although I have enquired, my friends still living in China have been unable to ascertain the how the artist has progressed.

One of our teachers was from Pakistan. He was a wonderful man, a fabulous teacher. We also had an ESL teacher from India, I will call her H. She was gentle and patient with the children and every day she came to school in colorful brocade clothing that looked like an exquisite painting. Knowing about the friction that existed between India and Pakistan, I was concerned about mixing them up when we had our first parent-student-teacher activity. And, of course, I did just that. You should have heard the gasp from the audience when I said the teacher from India was Pakistani! But they were good sports and forgave me for my terrible faux pas! As it turned out, we still keep in touch with our Pakistani teacher Mr. N. When NSCL closed, H lao shu and her husband opened an East Indian restaurant on the west side of town. I heard it was very successful. (BTW, did you notice you knew what lao shu meant? Look at you, you're learning Chinese! Han hao!)

Mr. N was a fine teacher. He taught secondary science – for inquiring minds. Kids could hardly wait to get to his class. There was no scientific question that he was not ready to create a situation where the class could seek the answers. The environment was stimulating. It was Myth Busters in the flesh! I have to admit I spent an inordinate amount of time in that classroom. His wife taught at one of the other international schools and was as delightful as he.

One of the Chinese teachers, B, taught Science (with Mr. N) and math. He was another outstanding teacher. Students loved to have him for math. He had a natural gift for making every moment a teachable one. When I had lunch in the teacher's lounge, B would always review Chinese vocabulary with me.

Star: We didn't lack for drama in our staff, either. The school was an American school, but with a twist. We taught ESL to our international students, but we also taught all the children Chinese. After all, they were living in China. We hired a Chinese CSL teacher for the lower grades. She was kind and patient with the children, and they made good progress under her tutelage. But two of the other Chinese teachers didn't like her for some reason. They fabricated a story about how she snooped in their classrooms, and they suspected her of taking their materials. They had no evidence to corroborate their claims, and I was disinclined to believe they were true. They settled into an uneasy truce, but I know they undermined her when the opportunity arose. The Business Manager (Chinese) was in my office on a regular basis to encourage me, with much eyebrow raising and innuendo to let her go. I held fast. And I never did learn what the real scoop. Bill and I had dinner with her and her husband several times. Her husband was military and was a student at Bei Da (the university). Bill was certain he was involved in something shady or was spying for the government. What did I say about biases! I don't believe that was true, but now and then I wonder. . .

In the meantime, Bill and I hired that very teacher to be our Chinese tutor. We had Chinese lessons weekly. She became a close friend. When we returned to China in 2010, we were able to reconnect and catch up. Star had a daughter who was able to secure a visa to go to college in the U.S. She was accepted at Duke. Star connected with us to let us know when they would be coming to the States. It was our intention to fly in and get together with Star and her daughter (Star was to be allowed to accompany her on a visitor's visa). The meeting never materialized. We inquired but were unable to find out whether the girl actually enrolled in Duke. Shortly after that, Star's email address stopped working. In the years since, we have never been able to reestablish contact.

On another occasion, one of the Chinese teachers came into my office and announced she needed the next two days off school. She explained she was going in to the doctor for an abortion, since she already had a child. I was already aware that in China, especially the urban areas, the law restricted couples to only one child, regardless of whether it was a girl or a boy. The Chinese favored boys, and I'm sure you have heard stories of female children being left out in the fields to die. That is frowned upon these days, although in very rural areas, that infanticide is still practiced. The law was actually more relaxed for rural areas, because farmers needed more children to work on the farm. I traveled back and forth to Beijing several times, and on each trip to the States there was a contingent of American adoptive parents with their newly adopted Chinese children. It was interesting to note the babies adopted by the foreign couples were almost always girls.

Ms. B: Soon after I arrived at NSCL, I was tasked with hiring some new teachers. One was an ESL teacher for elementary school. The lady we settled on was an American from my home State, Colorado. She arrived in Beijing late in August with two small children – 2 and 5 – in tow. We met her at the airport and took the family to their new apartment in Haidian, near several of the other teachers. The apartment was furnished, and we had arranged for some staples and food to be stocked for their use. The next day we took them shopping for other items and gave them a tour of the area.

Ms. B was a wonderful teacher. Her children were adorable. The youngest went to day care and the older child enrolled in kinder at NSCL. We became close friends and when the girls' grandmother passed away, we did our best to step in to try to fill the role. We enjoyed seeing them grow up, graduate and go to college, then move into the world of work when we all returned to Colorado. Ms. K has since fostered many children and adopted 4 additional children who call us Grandma Janet and Grandpa Bill. We love keeping up with their adventures, more often online now than in person. One has graduated from high school and moved to a group-living situation on the reservation. Three are in elementary and middle school. Another elementary-aged child has recently joined the group.

Ms. T was as office tech. She reminded me of Marilyn in Northern Exposure. She was tiny in stature, but she had that same knowing smile. She would listen and smile, listen and smile. She would answer your question and smile. She was a godsend. She knew what to do. She knew how to take care of business. And her Chinese was impeccable. She was always ready to prepare a note for me, in Chinese characters, for me to give my driver, my cabbies, or a parent, telling them where I wanted to go, when I needed to be there, or when we were going to meet. She was a great help to me as I acclimated to the responsibilities of my position.

Julia: I also had an Executive Assistant who was marvelous. Julia was beautiful, perfectly dressed and poised to make the best impression on visitors, parents, and professionals alike. Julia made them all feel welcome and important. She came to me out of the big business world where she was an executive secretary.

She spoke Mandarin and Cantonese, beautiful English, and passable Korean. She took on the role of translator when I was working with a Korean group. She was also culturally adept and understood the cultural nuances of different groups. She willingly shared her knowledge with me to help facilitate the flow of gatherings.

I recall one meeting with some Korean parents who were telling me of their financial hardships and how they just couldn't pay the balance of their children's tuition unless they could have an extension. Julia had prepped me by telling me the Korean families typically tried to bargain down their obligations. If they didn't get anywhere with the financial manager, they immediately wanted to meet with the HOS to see if they could get a more favorable answer. The reality was, they had the money to pay but it was hard to get it out of them. During the meeting, I commiserated with them. I understood how important their honor was to them. Using my American style, which I was sure was bumbling, I cautiously moved them to the direction of being glad to pay. I told them how much I appreciated their change of heart and apologized to them, hoping I had not offended them in any way by my American manners. When they left, Julia cried. "That was beautiful," she said. "You were so kind and respectful; they couldn't bear to let you down! You are learning and understanding us."

It wasn't all just business with Julia, either. We had a lot of fun together. She liked to take me places so I could learn more about China. Once she took me to her parent's home for lunch. I devoured the wonderful Chinese dumplings (joudza) her mother prepared especially for us. Then her father talked to me about Mao and what China was like under his regime. One day she took me to lunch at a joudza restaurant and negotiated with the cook to sell me a bamboo steamer I fancied. She and the cook thought I was crazy, and they laughed uproariously during the negotiation. The cook gave us extra dumplings at no charge! Julia still lives in Beijing. We had lunch with her when we returned to Beijing and Mongolia for a visit, and she and I keep in touch through email.

Jiang Hong was an upper school CSL (Chinese as a Second Language) teacher. Think of the hardest foreign language teacher you ever had in high school. Now double that. Wow! Every time I observed her, I was glad Bill and I had hired Star the Relentless for our private tutor. Jiang Hong introduced me to Chinese tea. One Saturday we took the Ching Way to the First Ring Road (downtown). We walked to a tea shop. The walls were lined with teas. The display tables were covered with teas. There were tea sets of every shape and size; costly to inexpensive. There were more flavors than I had ever dreamed existed.

We were escorted to a room of small covered tables and given menus. Of course, everything was in Chinese. Jiang Hong translated for me, and we selected a green tea, chrysanthemum, and ba bao cha (eight treasurers tea). A large steaming tea pot was brought to the table. Jiang Hong poured the tea, along with leaves, into our cups. "Just sip slowly," she instructed. The leaves should sink to the bottom. When we had finished the first tea, new cups and a brand-new tea pot appeared. This process was repeated for our third choice, as well. Later we wandered around the sales floor looking for items to purchase. I bought tea sets for each of our girls and a box of Eight Treasure Tea, my favorite.

Mr. Z, the HOS Emeritus, was challenging to work with. When I was hired, the school's owner kept him on to guide me. In his mind, that meant he was to continue to run the school. I had other ideas. He was still in the States when the Finance Director brought the need to move the school to me. We had two options - start school in the old building, run for a week, close school for a week while we moved, then reopen in the new facility, or start school in the new building two weeks late. We had many decisions to make, and solicited feedback from the Board and parents, as necessary, and finally determined to start the school year two weeks late. The Board and parents thought the late start was a better option, although it meant being in school for two extra weeks in the spring. Everyone was on board and the process began. The contract was signed, the renovations were initiated. Packing began, and fliers were sent out to parents and other schools.

The Head of School Emeritus returned to Beijing about 3 weeks prior to the start of school. He stormed into to my closet, slammed his hands on the desk, leaned in so his anger-reddened face was inches from mine and shouted, "You can't do that." "It's already done," I said calmly, "and it's all going to be fine." He stormed out of my office, and I could hear him ranting at the Business Director. Our plans continued undisturbed, but there was lots of grumbling about how it was never going to work. Of course it did work. Students and teachers enjoyed having an extra two weeks of summer and the extra days in the spring didn't seem to cause anyone problems.

Staff meetings were another challenge. I had observed a meeting on my first visit to Beijing. It amounted to the HOSE telling staff about what was going to be done, with no opportunity for staff input. I was (and still am) a great believer in having conversations and hearing everyone's ideas. The HOSE's method was much too dictatorial for me.

At our first staff meeting of the year, the HOSE jumped right in and began pontificating. I waited until he was finished. I stopped the group, welcomed everyone, introduced myself and explained how I would like to approach staff meetings and asked for input. I referred them to the written agenda on the tables in front of them. The HOSE argued. He said meetings were just to give the staff information and no one, especially the Chinese teachers, was going to give their opinions. I provided the group with a different view of the purpose of our meetings, suggesting that I wanted input from staff and healthy discussions about direction for the school. I wanted staff to be a part of the decision-making process. Again, an argument from the HOSE - no one would participate in discussions.

The other staff kindly agreed we should try my process. We continued the meeting. I suggested when there were discussion items, we could do a round robin. People could offer their opinion or pass. We would continue to move around the table until all staff could have their say and add to the discussion as they pleased. No one was allowed to interrupt or shut down the speaker. People could respond to a speaker when it was their turn. Then we would make a decision together on the direction we would take. My Assistant, Julia, would take notes. Our first discussion was about how the new facility was working for them and whether we needed to do any tweaking. The first four staff passed, a couple offered their thoughts, more passes, a complaint, an interruption from the HOSE attacking the complaint/complainant, a reminder about talking out of turn, more passes. At the end of the first go round, we recapped the ideas that had been expressed. Then suddenly, on the second go round, everyone wanted to talk. The HOSE still burst in a couple of times to shut down a speaker and had to be admonished. Everyone got a chance to be heard. We had a very successful meeting and left discussing all the new ideas we had generated and were poised to work on. The staff was happy with the arrangement and glad to have their opinions considered and incorporated into the life of the school. The HOSE became less of a challenge as time went on. Staff meetings became an exciting exchange of thoughts and ideas.

I was fortunate to have or to hire some excellent teaching staff. Some had been at the school for several years; some were new transplants. They were a part of the international school community of educators, an adventurous group who taught for a while in one country and then moved on to the next. During my tenure, three of them moved on. I wrote them a light-hearted going-away poem to celebrate their time with us.

I realized much later the poem was a reflection of my husband and my experiences in China. It was an expression of the many challenges we faced during our stay.

Fare Well

You set out on a different path.
You came to China; learned new math.
You brought us knowledge – precious jewel,
And joined the team at our New School.
The students said, "You're really cool!"

You walked the river's length and more.
You took the bus to every store.
Faced frightening times with calm and poise;
Shared students' triumphs, pain, and joys;
Unveiled new worlds for girls and boys.

You trekked 'cross country, kids in tow.
You taught the students; watched them grow;
Brought wit and wisdom, wrote and drew;
Put on the colors gold and blue;
Listened, graded, counseled, too.

And now you leave for far away;
Kuwait, Eugene, or old Bombay.
To you, the best we all relay;
Good thoughts to speed you on your way. And
hopes to meet another day.

American Holiday In A Far-away Land: We Are Definitely NOT in Kansas Anymore

Hong Dou Sha (houng doe shah) Red Bean Paste

We love the excitement and romance of travel, but actually moving away from family and friends is a wrench. And moving to another country presents its share of challenges. We could not just hit the road and drive home from China. Flying was expensive and time consuming. But there we were in Beijing, and Thanksgiving was fast approaching! So, like the bulk of our teachers, we prepared to celebrate Thanksgiving in China.

Bill and I decided to host a Thanksgiving get-together for our staff. Turkey, however, is not a Chinese staple. We couldn't get turkey. (Actually, we could have had it imported, but two factors dissuaded us. One, it was extremely expensive and other Westerners who had done it didn't offer rave reviews. Two, at a function hosted by the American Embassy, I had tasted the imported turkey, which was like a roast pressed around what was called dressing and then sliced. I had to agree with the other reviewers, so we passed.)

We couldn't get pumpkin, either. It was not grown in China, we were told, and in support of that telling we actually never encountered it. Fortunately, one fall afternoon, when we were on an outing to the Ming Tombs, we encountered produce stands by the side of the road. One stand had orange-colored squashes that reminded me a little of Sultan's Turban squash. I purchased two, which were about the size of 8" pumpkins. We cleaned and baked the squash. We mashed the flesh, added spices and created mini "pumpkin" pies in our tiny toaster oven (Chinese kitchens do not typically have ovens. I found a tiny toaster oven at a Chinese department store). The filling was more pink than orange, but homemade crust and the whipped cream on top saved the day!

We found cans of Ocean Spray Cranberry Sauce at Jenny Lou's market. We bought deviled quail eggs and a variety of potato chips. We decided because cold cuts were available (including turkey) and recognizable, we would try to create fancy sandwiches. For "fancy" we intended to use croissants. On one trip to the grocery store, we had discovered them. Beautiful just like they had come straight from the boulangerie! And they were delicious! The day before the party, we went to buy several dozen so they would be fresh.

On party morning, we set about slicing the croissants and discovered most of them were filled with red bean paste, a kind of jam of mashed beans, sugar, and grease. Not a happy surprise. It was too late to change plans. We stood with the wastebasket between us and scooped the paste out of all those croissants! As we shared our misstep with staff, one of our Chinese guests pointed out how the Chinese characters explained which were plain and which were filled. Later, I made it a point to learn the characters for bean paste so we could avoid it. That isn't to say we didn't eat it at all. During Chinese New Year, we often had moon cakes filled with it, and they were quite tasty. Tuna fish mixed with it, however, got only one star!

In the end, the sandwiches were fine, and the mini pumpkin pies were a hit. The American contingent shared with our colleagues what our relatives back in the states were doing to celebrate Thanksgiving and learned some interesting facts about celebrations in China, India, Pakistan and Canada. We were all thankful to have one another's company - for many of us, as strangers in a strange land.

I remember my daughter Amy telling us how our family went out together to a restaurant that fall for Thanksgiving dinner, but it just didn't compare to the feasts we'd always had at home together with home-made everything, and no bean paste of any color!

The Business End of International Schools

Xuefei (shoe eh fay) Tuition

As a private school, we charged tuition and fees for our services. Our school was registered with the Chinese government, but it had irregularities. It had been founded by an American woman and a Chinese businessman. It was a convoluted story of intrigue and secrecy and betrayal, but the government recognized the school as belonging to the businessman, when it was supposed to have been handed over to the American woman. An item of great interest for the Board was to negotiate with the businessman and secure the school's "chops" so we could operate at the highest level of openness possible.

You might be wondering what "chops" are. The Chinese chop is like a seal or an official stamp. They can be for personal or business use and are a popular souvenir. Chops are small, about the same size as a signature or date stamp in the US, and can be made from stone, plastic, metal, or wood. Organizations must apply for approval for a chop from the Public Security Bureau. A personal chop is a signature stamp (in Chinese characters, of course). It is used instead of signing one's name. A company chop is a legally binding stamp. Chops are used on invoices, for bank transactions, and to sign official documents. A business without chops is not a state-recognized organization.

As it was, because we had no chops to open bank accounts, the Financial Officer ran the financial end of the school through his private bank account. All the tuition money flowed through his coffers. As an American administrator, I was very uncomfortable with that arrangement, as he was the person in charge of collecting tuition and managing and tracking revenue and expenditures, as well. But the Board had been operating for several years with that arrangement, so it stayed in place. The Board Chair and I spent several months trying to negotiate with the businessman who had our school's chops. He was actually very affable fellow who had simply invested a good deal of money in the school with the promise that he would realize some type of profit. We had several conversations with him pleading our case. I'm not sure whether he really understood why schools should be a different animal than other businesses, or he just got tired of listening to us. But, finally, he conceded to hand over the chops as a contribution, instead of taking the monetary kickback he really wanted. I still recall the day in early June when Julia and I went to the bank to officially open accounts under the name of the school and transferred our funds to those accounts.

The school operated on the tuition paid by students. That funding paid for teachers' and staffs' salaries, school materials, teacher housing, rental of school facilities, school buses, and maintenance, etc. The Business Manager secured apartments for teachers that were adequate, if not impressive. They were furnished; they had modern bathrooms and washing machines. When a new teacher was hired, the school also provided them with a week's worth of basic groceries and a bouquet of flowers. Of course, assistance in getting around and getting set up with other necessities was also provided. For teachers, paid housing was a wonderful benefit.

CHAPTER 6

Gobi Sand and Camel Hair

At NSCL THERE WERE THREE EDUCATIONAL EXCURSIONS PER YEAR. In the fall, seniors were set to go to the 3-gorges dam to study the impact of the project on the local citizenry and ecology. They traveled by train and then by boat on the Yangtze. It was a trip I hated to miss, but as a new administrator, I felt I needed to be at the school.

The previous spring, third graders had gone to work with Dr. Pan at the Panda Refuge in Chengdu. Dr. Pan came to the school in the fall to update the children (now fourth graders) on the continuing results of their research. Dr Pan looked a lot like the creatures he studied and protected - deep-set eyes, with dark circles, a short, sturdy, dough-boy body. He looked gentle and curious, yet powerful. With the help of Lady C, as translator, the staff and children had a wonderful visit with him. In the evening, the school hosted a dinner honoring him.

Third graders were planning a trip to Mongolia to investigate the culture of the nomads and Mongolian schools. The husband of the third-grade teacher had an NGO in Mongolia. His parents were missionaries. They had funded the NGO in Mongolia, and Dr. Oods had inherited it from them. It was funded by the Presbyterian church, although no overt proselytizing was allowed. Instead, the missionaries brought and distributed educational and medical materials. Dr. Oods spoke passable Mongolian, and he had developed many contacts there over the years. That was the trip Bill and I selected to participate in as chaperones. It turned out to be the trip of a lifetime!

Riding the Train to Mongolia

We met at the Beijing train station just after dawn on a chilly April day with our baggage. When all adults and children were accounted for and goodbyes were said, we marched to the train and climbed aboard. Bill and I were assigned to be the chaperones to two boys, Adam and Olam. The boys were as different as day and night, but they were best friends. Adam was Chinese/American. He was neat, organized and serious. Olam was from New Guinea. He was carefree, messy and happy. They were inseparable. They were both adorable!

As the train pulled out for our 22-hour trip, the boys went to join another group and one of the staff came to sit with us. The train moved at a snail's pace, proceeding up the mountains on switch backs. Forward and backward we went, inching up the incline.

At noon, everyone broke out their sack lunches. We got water for tea and Ramen noodles from the boiler in the vestibule. The boiler was constantly monitored by an attendant. Everyone in the car had their container to get water and either use it hot for tea or let it cool to refill water bottles. Adults secured the water for the children from the super-heated boiler to protect them from getting burned. For dinner, we walked to the dining car.

At bedtime, the concierge came around and made up the berths, two upper and two lower. The children took the upper berths. The blankets were made of camel hair and were thick and warm. Later, I tried to buy one from the concierge, who looked at me like I had lost my mind. No matter how I tried she would not budge from "no". (We got our camel hair blanket after all, though, when the Oods sent us a beautiful one for Christmas. I'm sure securing it included a story to tell!)

As we neared the Mongolian border, we were awakened and informed we would have a 6-hour "lay-over" while passports were checked, and the wheels of the train were changed. There would be no bathroom access during that period. Everyone would need to use the bathroom right away and go back to their own compartment.

After arriving at the border, the long wait began. First Chinese customs and passport officials came through the cabins. After the inspection was completed, the wheel change began. The gauges of the tracks in China and Mongolia are different so the wheels are changed when the trains go across the border. I was told the reason for the different gauges was the result of past invasions. The Chinese wanted to stop any invasions into the country by train. The tedious process started with all the cars being separated from one another and put in this long building. Then hoists were put under the cars, and they were lifted up. One set of wheels was removed from under the train car and another set was attached. All of this took about 3 hours.

When we were back on the ground and reattached, Mongolian customs and passport control boarded the train. More time, waiting. Finally, at about 2:00 in the morning we were on our way to Sianshand.

As a sidenote, Chinese customs officials are thorough in their work because they are worried about Chinese citizens defecting to other countries. We were told that they frequently searched above the drop ceilings and under the compartment beds. And they did sometimes find stowaways. The Mongolian officials were not nearly as focused, although they pondered a long time on children's passports from New Guinea and South Korea.

The train arrived at Sainshand as dawn was beginning to paint the sky. It was about 15 degrees below zero with a light breeze that was a real wake-up call after the warmth of the train (and those wonderful blankets!). All around us was sand – no trees or bushes; no buildings other than the depot; no pavement. The transportation to our hotel arrived and off we went.

The buses transporting us were Russian made station wagons. They reeked of raw gasoline, and we struggled to cram 20 people with luggage into the two of them. The drive to our destination was short, and soon we had arrived at the hotel. The hotel was brick and looked like an American building from the 50's. It seemed modern enough

We are assigned a room with Olumb and Aaron. The room had a wooden table with 4 chairs and 4 beds. The beds appeared to be old military cots and when Bill sat down on one, the metal springs sank to the floor. He laid down and his feet hung off the end. It didn't look like we'd be very comfortable, but at least the room was warm and there were those wonderful camel hair blankets again.

The next day we went to meet the Governor of the East Gobi Province. He had complete say over what we would be allowed to do. It was interesting that in this small town with shabby-looking Russian built buildings and crumbling road paving due to lack of resources, the Governor was educated in Czechoslovakia and held a PhD. He obviously liked the Oods, and he was very accommodating. He weighed us down with gifts. They included a hand made camel rug depicting a famous Mongolian philosopher, which we still have today.

(We learned later our hotel belonged to the Governor, and that he made sure that the food we got was more western than Mongolian. He was concerned the kids would have a hard time with the local cuisine. Whatever it was, the food was delicious.)

Next, we went to the local elementary school and were introduced to the principal. Then we went to a classroom with kids the same age as ours. It was bedlam. After lunch, more time with children in the classrooms. The teachers collaborated to teach the group about interesting cultural similarities and differences. That evening, after the children were fed, the adults were invited to have dinner with the Governor.

After breakfast the next day we all piled into the Russian-made vehicles and the Governor's Toyota 4runner and headed for the Gobi Desert. Our journey took us first to a Buddhist Temple. On the way we came across a herd of goats and camels at a well. We stopped and the nomads let us ride a camel and one of their horses. Camels, as you know are Bactrian, the kind with two humps, and the Mongolian horses are smaller than a quarter horse. The Mongolians are superb horsemen, and boys begin riding at an early age. The saddle is made to allow the rider to stand in the stirrups. Horse races are a popular pastime. We saw intricately worked saddles and tack at a local marketplace, but given our rather primitive setting, we didn't purchase anything.

The Buddhist Temple site had been there for a long time. When the Russians occupied the country, they burned all of the original buildings, but since they left in 1990, reconstruction had begun. It was a slow process due to lack of funds.

Next, we went to a geological site that had petrified trees. Some of them were 2 or more feet in diameter. Then to a fossil area, but no one found any fossils. We did find many lovely small rocks, and everyone was allowed to take a few. After that we went back to the temple area and had lunch in a school that served the monk's families. The governor had sent his personal kitchen crew out with us to cook. After lunch we went to a well and watched the Mongolian nomad herders water their animals. Finally, we went to some sand dunes and then back to town.

The next day the children went to another elementary school with their teachers. My husband went off with Dr. Oods to look at infrastructure, and I went to the high school to confer with officials about American educational practices. Schools in China and Mongolia were typically rote learning environments. Students sat at their desks. They read out loud with the teacher. The teacher lectured. The teacher administered tests. The Mongolian government was interested in adopting a more Western approach, and we had lively discussions about American practices. In the end, we promised to send instructional materials to support our counterparts in working with teachers. .

In the afternoon, I observed classes and taught an English as a Second Language (ESL) lesson to sophomores. There was lots of embarrassed giggling as they tried TPR (Total Physical Response), but the students became engaged quickly enough, and we had a delightful couple of hours.

Dr. and Mrs. Oods

I could have written about Mrs. Oods when I discussed some of the school's teachers. However, Mrs. Oods and her husband figured so prominently in our experience in China, I felt they needed a chapter of their own. Below is a bit of their story.

The school's second/third grade teacher was from the United States but had lived most of her adult life in China. She spoke the language well. Her husband had been a university professor. They had grown children who also lived in China, and grandchildren, as well. Mrs. Oods was a very proper southern lady. Her poise and grace fit perfectly in the Chinese environment. She was consulted by other teachers. Her council was trusted, by myself, as well. In the classroom, she was a pro. The children were always interested and engaged. Even when the classroom seemed filled with hubbub, one could see that it was purposeful, and learning was taking place.

Mr. Oods often volunteered at our school and brought science activities and experiments to his wife's class. He also taught tennis to elementary and secondary kids as a part of the extracurricular program. When he found out I could play tennis he enlisted me as an assistant coach.

Originally, I thought their last name was Oods, misunderstanding the pronunciation of Woods by the school secretaries, whose native tongue was Chinese. The Oodses were a great addition to the school. As I have discussed elsewhere in this book, the first fall we were in Beijing, the second/third grade class was scheduled to take a one-week educational field trip. Dr. and Mrs. Woods had an NGO (Non-governmental Organization) based out of their US church to assist the East Gobi Province with education, medical supplies and information, and, of course, as possible, religion.

Dr. Oods arranged the trip for the class. The trip included educational activities in the schools of the city of Sainshand, cultural exchanges with the Chinese students, a music and dance festival, and visits to various groups of Nomads to learn about and participate in their lives. As the Oods-proclaimed "administration expert", I participated in meetings with the Governor and principals to discuss educational theory and provide live illustrations of western teaching styles. I also spent one delightful afternoon teaching English to Mongolian high school students to demonstrate interactive learning and TPR. My husband was dubbed the "agricultural expert" and spent his days assisting Dr. Oods with helping the locals understand and implement new ag technologies.

Long after we left China, the Oods remained, teaching and spreading good will. They finally retired and returned to the States sometime around the Covid 19 pandemic. We still keep in touch.

The Wild West

We arrived at Sainshand, the capital of the East Gobi Province, in the early morning. Everyone was happy to get off the train and walk around. My first impressions of the town are my most lasting. There was a town square with formal-looking, brick, government buildings. There were two dirt roads that intersected in the middle of town. There were no stop signs or traffic lights. There were concrete sidewalks around the government buildings, and around some schools and businesses, but not all. There were people moving back and forth, walking, on horseback (nomads), on bikes, and an occasional car. The air was clean and crisp; the sky was a turquoise canvas overhead. It made me think of a Western film.

The hotel was close by, and we headed for it. It was small and rustic, but clean. Our group was divided up into three rooms, girls and female teachers in one large dormitory room, boys and male teachers in another, and Bill and I with our two charges – Adam and Olam – in a third. The beds were old Russian army issue with thin mattresses thrown over metal springs. When my husband lay down, the springs stretched enough that his fanny hit the floor. The beds were short, so he had to scrunch so his feet wouldn't hang off the edge. Blankets, however, were made of thick, cozy, warm camel wool. Wonderful! There were a few other small rooms that housed additional guests.

There was one bathroom that served all guests. It had two stalls and a sink. One of the toilets was out of order. There were no showers. There was a small dining room where we took our meals, since there few restaurants in the town. The hotel was considered 4-star and was owned by our host, the Governor of the East Gobi province, as I mentioned before. It was actually the only hotel in town.

We returned to Sainshand 8 years later and were amazed to find several hotels and restaurants, as well as an increased number of cars sharing the roads with horsemen in their traditional clothing. There was a "stop light". It was hanging over the middle of the dirt crossroads. As I recall, it flashed red or green.

During that second stay, we met with the Governor once more. He was serious and businesslike, but also very welcoming. He showered us with gifts and was personally involved in arranging activities for us and sending his personal chefs with us to prepare our meals. He made sure we were able to witness a nomad parade and had tickets to an evening concert – complete with acrobats, contortionists and throat singing. The Oods explained to us that he had been recently promoted, which probably meant he would move to the capital. I wonder today, so many years later, where his path took him and whether his successor was as forward thinking.

Trekking Across the Gobi in Russian Jeeps

The Governor arranged transportation and drivers for excursions. We rode in old Russian jeeps that reeked of gasoline and broken-down Volkswagen buses. On one excursion we traveled out onto the Gobi Desert to a site covered with the remains of a forest – now petrified wood. The teachers spent the morning conducting scientific activities with the children and I gathered up a bag of sand. I couldn't believe I was walking around on the Gobi Desert. I wanted to take some sand home with me.

We had a "picnic" lunch out on blankets spread over the sand, again courtesy of the Governor. Then we headed down the road to one of the public wells in the region. When I say, "down the road", you need to understand there were no paved roads. We traveled down a dirt track – nothing formal, no signs to guide your way, just the drivers who knew where they were going. Of course, there wasn't much automobile traffic outside of the cities, and the nomads rode horses or camels. When we returned 8 years later, we anticipated paved roads would have been constructed, but we were wrong. The road from Sainshand to Ulaanbaatar was still an unpaved dirt track, and the nomads were still riding their horses and camels.

While trekking through the Gobi, we came to a watering place, a well that had been dug and improved for use by the herdsmen. There was a large band of nomads watering their animals. Mongolian nomads are herders. Typically, they travel with 5 herds. They have their Bactrian camels (two humps – much easier to ride than the Dromedary of Saharan fame), their horses (small and sturdy), cattle, goats, and sheep. The valley before us was littered with the herds. Some of the nomads were shepherding and directing herd movements to and from the well. Others were working the pumps to draw the water up to the troughs so the animals could drink.

Suddenly there was an uproar. Coming down onto the valley floor was a group of five wild camels. There humps were flopped over, demonstrating the animal's need to food and water. They had come to gorge on water, to fill their now depleted humps.

The nomads leaped into action. Some continued to fill the water troughs while others rounded up their herds and moved them away from the well. The wild camels came into the well area and began to drink. When they had their fill and left, the nomads returned their herds to the well.

When I asked why that had been done, I was told the nomads had great love and respect for the wild camels, and always made sure they had first place at the wells. The Mongolian wild camel is considered to be Critically Endangered, with only about 7 to 8 hundred in existence. Interestingly, the wild Bactrian camel is said to be a different species from the domestic Bactrian camel, although they are very similar in appearance. The wild camels can drink highly salty water and can process snow for water. Of course, the Mongolian nomad depends on his camels. The hair can be used to make garments, blankets, and rope. The animals are used for transportation and carrying. The milk and meat are also used.

I had never been close up and personal with a Bactrian camel before going to Mongolia, but I can tell you they are delightful creatures. They are quite gentle. They have large, expressive eyes with extremely long eyelashes. I'm sure the eyelashes protect them from blowing sand, but they also give them quite a glamorous appearance. When you talk to them, they look at you and bat those big baby-browns as if they totally understand and agree. They love to be scratched behind their ears, on their necks and behind their front legs. They do have great oversized feet, more like snowshoes than feet, again in response to the environment, and they are very heavy if they step on yours! When you wish to ride, they will kneel for you, and you can climb up into the saddle between their humps. I loved how secure riding between the humps made you feel, no matter how fast you were going.

Mongolian Hygiene and Eating Habits

Let me begin this story on an early morning at the community bath house. The temperature is 17 degrees, but the sun is warming. We have all walked the 4 blocks to the bath house for our weekly shower. The bath house is divided into two areas – one for women and one for men. The women's area is divided into a common room and three communal showers. There are benches in the common room on which we set our belongings, clothes and shoes. The floors and benches are wet. There is a large electric motor at one end. We are cautioned not to touch the unit so as not to get a shock. We divide the children into groups and send them into the showers to wash. Each child has a small bar of soap (brought from home). When the children are done, they sit on the benches and wait for the teachers. We exit the building with damp clothes, damp hair and damp bodies. The children are hustled back to the hotel down the street to get warm.

Showered and semi-dried, I am sitting on the front steps of the facility looking at the traffic going in and out of the local market in front of me. A man parks his three-wheeled bike near the door and lifts an enormous sheep off the carrier on the back. He leads the animal into the market. More people come and go, and, of course, I am interested in going into it at least for a tour. The three-wheeled bike man staggers out of the market under a huge weight. He proceeds to load and arrange huge pieces of something into the basket. Suddenly I realize they are haunches of meat. I am looking at the sheep that he has brought to be slaughtered. My Interest in touring the market has vanished.

I note this to say that the Mongolians eat a great deal of mutton, in addition to beef, camel, and goat. Refrigeration exists, but electricity is not dependable in remote areas. We often ate in restaurants or were provided food in businesses where the smell of poorly refrigerated mutton permeated. We tried to work around it, but sometimes it was just impossible to eat without gagging. For sheltered Americans, it was as repulsive as chicken heads in the soup, or whole baked fish with eyes.

In less modernized areas like Sainshand was when we first were there, Western modes of serving restaurant customers were non-existent. At one such restaurant, 20 of us were seated to have lunch. It was 11:30. The waitress appeared and took the order for one of our party. Fifteen minutes later, she returned with the meal for that person. Then she took the order from the next one. Fifteen minutes later, she returned with their food. And so on and so on until the final person was served. Then she started at the beginning to take drink orders. Needless to say, the people who were first to order had long finished their meal before the last people were served. We all passed on ordering dessert.

Riding the Wild Camel

As we traveled about with the children, we stopped at a nomad camp. The herdsman had several camels, as well as goats and sheep. Camels were prepared for riding. They were commanded to kneel, and children were lifted onto their backs, seated between the humps. Mongolian herdsmen walked them out into the desert and back again. Teachers were allowed to ride on their own, although herdsmen rode with the group, I suspected for safety's sake, as well. Some teachers went galloping across the sand. Everyone enjoyed the activity.

I was enchanted by the appearance of the Bactrian camel. They have beautiful eyes with long eyelashes. In Gobi dust storms, these eyelashes offer significant protection for the eyes. Their faces are quite gentle, and they love a good scratch behind their ears. There is ample room to sit between the two humps for a ride. The knees are knobby, and the feet are enormous. It made me sad to see the huge bone spike that pierced their nose and attached to the rein that was used to steer them or make them kneel. Many of them complained vociferously at the effort, sending forth loud grunts of irritation. Others simply knelt down when their owner touched and spoke to them.

My husband got involved in a "conversation" with one of the herdsmen about how well he rode, and his background as a country boy. The man decided to give Bill the camel he was riding. He said he would care for the beast, but any time Bill came back, the camel was there for his use. If he wanted to take it with him at any time, it was his for the taking. (All this was done through Mr. Oods, and our interpreter, Tumai. Bill was quite touched. He often shares the story of how he owns a camel that lives with nomads on the Gobi Desert.

Mrs. Ood's Special Guest

Hotel arrangements in Sainshand for the class trip to Mongolia included Mrs. Oods staying with a small group of girls in a room near the front desk and lobby.

It was late on our first night there. Everyone was tired from the train trip (22 hours) and from the activities we had already taken part in. The temperature had rapidly dropped below zero. We had all gone to bed. The hotel was quiet. Mrs. Oods was awakened to someone trying to climb into her bed with her. She realized at once it was a male nomad who was quite drunk. He was still fully dressed, including his hat and coat. She leapt to her feet and slipped out silently to get her husband. Mr. Oods came quickly, and the two of them were able to extract the gentleman from the bed and usher him to a bench in the lobby without disturbing the children. He was still there, sound asleep, when we all came out for breakfast. By the time we returned from our adventures that afternoon, he was gone.

The children were none the wiser for the incident, but the rest of us teased Mrs. Oods mercilessly about her new boyfriend, even when we returned to NSCL. The boyfriend did not return on subsequent nights, so we speculated he was on his way somewhere and just sought a warm place for the night.

Ulaanbaatar

The second time we went to Mongolia was markedly different than the first. We flew into Beijing, then took a second flight to Ulaanbaatar, Mongolia. We were met at the airport and taken to the Korean Embassy's Korean Guest House to get settled in.

As I noted before, Dr. Oods had an NGO in Mongolia. It was underwritten by the Presbyterian church. On this trip we were basically good will missionaries (not religious). There were several other volunteers traveling with us. Some of them were college students. We all met with the Oods at the Korean Guest House to learn the details of our trip. The suitcases filled with children's school supplies and small toys were handed over to our group leaders to be organized. We learned we would be typically taking continental breakfast at our lodging, sharing picnic lunches (food to be provided by the group leaders) and eating dinner at a restaurant. We had an itinerary for each day. When we were finished in Ulaanbaatar, we would travel to Sainshand and Altan Shiree. We met our Mongolian translator, Tumai. It was noted that the third location was not as welcoming to strangers, and we would need to carefully follow all rules, especially those around proselytizing.

Ulaanbaatar was fascinating. It was a large city. It was filled with museums, statues, including one commemorating Genghis Khan, historical sites, an enormous herdsman ger community, and, of course, shopping. As modern as it seemed in some ways, the paved streets were more pothole than paving and the sidewalks were crumbling. We were told that the discovery of many precious metals and resources had foreign interests beginning to invest heavily in opening up the economy, but currently, the country was isolated and relatively poor. We went to the bank to exchange our US dollars for Mongolian tugrik. We visited an open market, where we encountered many nomads selling handmade items. Beautiful saddles and tack for horses and camels. Items made from camel and sheep wool. We bought some smaller trinkets for family.

I want to stop here and share with the reader exactly what a "ger" is. A ger is a portable, round tent. They are designed to be easy to set up and take down. The Russians called them Yurts, which the Mongolians hated. When the Russian occupation ended, the Mongolians went back to calling them gers. Typically, a ger was made from flexible, lightweight wood and sheep and camel products. A heavy felt was woven from camel hair and made into panels. Sheep's wool was used for insulation. The panels formed the walls and ceiling of the dwelling. (The same felt was made into warm boots, as well). Often animal hides covered the walls, and horsehair ropes held the roof and walls in place. The dome at the top is called a toono and is considered sacred. It is said to connect the earth to the sky. It is often passed down from family member to family member. The floor was usually made of hard packed earth. Modern gers are also made from canvas and can have a wooden floor. When the nomads were ready to move locations, the ger was taken down quickly and packed into carts or onto animals' backs.

We visited the nomads. There were thousands of them, living in their gers, on the outskirts of the city. They had given up their herding life and moved their families to where they believed they could make a better life. There animals were gone and the old ways were dying. There was no electricity, no running water in the community.

We were invited into a family's home for tea. We sat politely on small wooden benches to one side of the dwelling while the hostess prepared the tea. First, the tea leaves (black tea) were added to a pot filled with water and camel's milk that had been heating over the fire. Sugar and spices were added. Then the tea was served in small bowls. (We had occasion to also try suutei tsai at another visit. Salt and toasted millet replaced the sugar and spices.) I was never a big tea drinker, but both beverages were tasty). Tumai and Dr. Oods had a long conversation with the family, and I just enjoyed looking at everything.

This particular ger had benches, and an adobe and metal cooking area in the middle, with a stovepipe that reached up to the ceiling. It was bright and cozy, as well as warm. It had the typical narrow tunnel-type entry way one had to bend over to enter, to help keep out the wind, sand and cold.

In Ulaanbaatar we stayed in a hostel rather than a hotel. The Korean Guest House where we stayed offered private rooms with baths. Fabulous, I thought. It was warm. It had beds. It was great to have a room with a shower! There was one drawback. We had one towel to share. It was the size of a hand towel. It was the kind of towel you can purchase at the discount store. Thin and unable to accommodate much water. So, the first showerer enjoyed a small, but dry, cloth to use. The second showerer had the same small, but now damp, cloth. It was quite comical, and there was nothing to do for it. There was a lot of air drying going on!

After an enlightening visit, we departed the Capital on the train. The train ride to Sainshand was long, but the landscape we passed, and the company were interesting. This time, however, we had no children to look after, we were only two in our compartment, and we were able to wander about and explore. Our activities in Sainshand were to be much like those of 9 years past – support for the schools, school and medical supplies for the nomads, and agricultural advice.

Ministering to Sainshand

We arrived in Sainshand. We couldn't believe how it had changed. There were two additional hotels and many restaurants. There were many more cars, and a great deal more activity. We were housed in one of the new hotels and our room was modern. We were told it had been modeled after western hotels. Unfortunately, it had what I will refer to as "Chinese" plumbing (I acknowledge and apologize for my personal bias and pettiness, but my Western nose and preferences overpower me in this situation.)

The shower had two walls covered with a variety of shower heads. It would seem that one could pick and choose to enjoy different levels of power and modality. The opening to the shower was, however, about 2 feet off the ground. It was almost impossible to climb into, and more than a little dangerous to life and limb (and other body parts). Once you managed to get in without maiming yourself, you discovered that none of the bells and whistles worked. And in order to get hot water out of the overhead nozzle, you had to have the hot water turned on in the sink. Really? I was back to shaking my head at plumbing!

The beds were also different. Wooden boxes, the height of a normal bed. A camel hair mat, approximately two inches thick. Blankets and a pillow. I've done a lot of camping in my life, and this was quite similar to sleeping in a bag on the ground. Bill, who is ex-military, and much harder than I, slept pretty well. Like a princess with a pea. I tossed and turned and even attempted to fold the mat in half, with limited success. I laughed at what a weenie I was, but it didn't make the bed softer.

Our tasks on this trip were similar to what we had done before. There were some differences. We visited what I would call a mission run by a Korean woman. We brought school and medical supplies. She had a small congregation. They were working on creating educational activities for children and for creating gardens. We provided support and some hard labor. It didn't take long to realize she was working zealously to impart religious instruction, as well. I noticed the Oodes spent a lot of time trying to tone down her rhetoric.

We visited with the Governor again, and he was very welcoming. The second evening, he arranged for us to attend a Mongolian concert. It was in a large concert hall with only one entrance. Scary, but ok, when in Rome. We were entertained by acrobats, dancers, contortionists, a nomad band, and throat singing. It was all so interesting.

After about 2 hours, Bill and I decided we were going back to the hotel to get some rest. The young people all remained and hoped to go "out on the town" afterwards. We had just walked into our room when the lights in the entire town went out. And they stayed out. We were concerned about our colleagues. Later they shared that it was pitch dark in the hall. Everyone had remained calm, however, and people started making their way slowly to the exit. It took a long time, because no one had flashlights (not even cell phones) to help them. The lights went back on sometime during the night.

Milking a Camel

One lovely morning we stopped at the gers of a group of nomads. The group had representation of all the "5 herds" - camels, horses, goats, sheep and cattle.

We were offered rides on camels, and several of the group accepted. I was more interested in a lady who was going to milk a camel. She beckoned me to join her. We stood next to the female, who was tethered. Her calf paced close by. The lady held her wooden bucket under the belly of the camel with one arm and milked with the other. I watched. Then she pressed the bucket into my arms and indicated I should give it a try. I had experience milking goats and cows, so it didn't take long to get acclimated, although it was strange to be standing rather than sitting on a stool. When we were done, she gave the bucket to a child to take to the ger.

The camels were shedding. She invited me to pull some of the wool that was beginning to slough from the camels. I soon had a small bundle of it. It was soft and warm. I thanked her – bayrl-laa. I took it back to Beijing with me and packed it in a gallon Ziploc bag. When we returned to the U.S. the final time, I packed it in my suitcase. Back in the States, I was showing it to a friend. "How did you ever get it through Customs?" she asked. I was surprised. It never occurred to me it was something that had to be declared and I had given it no thought. It wasn't confiscated, so maybe it wasn't a big deal.

Altan Shiree
An Uncomfortable Experience

The last city we were to visit was Altan Shiree. It was a morning's drive out in the Gobi. We all squeezed into a large, 12-passenger but and off we went down a dirt track road. The mission manager went with us. I hoped her zeal did not get us into trouble, as the Mongolians, like the Chinese, do not tolerate open proselytizing.

About an hour into the drive, the engine overheated. We stopped. The driver used all his spare water to fill the engine. We exited the bus and walked around and looked at the rocks and sparce fauna of the area.

Half an hour later, and we were back on the trail. The engine overheated again. This time we were asked to give up our individual bottles of water, because there was nowhere to get any. We complied. But I wondered about the efficacy of that move. There we were in the middle of the desert, now with no water, and in a vehicle that might or might not make it to our destination. We had passed no vehicles on the road. In fact, we had seen no one.

But, after a while we were again on the move. We made it to Altan Shiree by fits and starts. Hooray, I thought. Water (and food, actually, since we had brought none and everyone was getting hungry).

Altan Shiree was primitive. There was a kind of a trading post affair that had a few food items available. It was not prepared to accommodate a group as large as ours, and there was a great deal of negotiation about securing water and about fixing our vehicle, which had coasted into the town and quit. The buildings of the town were gray. There were no trees, no flowers, no hint of color or joy, except from the beautiful blue sky overhead. The people in the trading post were wary, and just about two steps from unfriendly. We got some food and went outside.

My husband went off with Dr. Oods to inspect the town's well. The town had spent a great deal of money to bring in a Western company to dig the well. The well worked fine for a time, but after a while the water it produced had turned bitter. It was so strong that it curdled the tea milk and made it taste bad.

I went to the school with the other volunteers. We worked with the teachers and provided them with a large donation of school supplies for the children. Our experience in the school was positive. The teachers and the children were delightful. We shared teaching strategies back and forth. We helped in the classrooms. We shared some strategies for working effectively with children with special needs.

Three of the young volunteers and I walked around looking for an outhouse. We discovered one and went about taking care of our needs. The inside of the outhouse was scary. The floor was a bunch of loose boards thrown down in front of a wooden seat. There were enormous gaps between the boards, sometimes a foot wide. You had to tread with care so as not to fall through. One of the girls dropped her $200 sunglasses down one of the gaps. She wanted one of the rest of us to reach down into the morass and help her retrieve them. We just looked at her. No one jumped at the chance to help. She refused to do it either. It was an expensive lesson.

We went back to the trading post to discover that the driver and someone in the town had been able to fix the bus. That was better than great, because there was nowhere to stay in the town. And even if there had been, I'm not sure we would have been welcome. The townspeople were angry. The mission lady had been discovered preaching, which was not acceptable. She had been brought back to the trading post and detained. The wary faces had become unfriendly. The atmosphere had become negatively charged. The Oodses were furious at her. As soon as everyone had assembled, we all got back on the bus and left for Sainshand. Fortunately, the bus fix worked, and we arrived safely in the evening.

I felt bad for the Oodses. They had invested many hours in their work with Altan Shiree. The mission lady had seriously damaged their reputation and relationship with the community. I wondered whether they would ever be invited back.

Return to Beijing

Another night on the torture bed, and we were ready to return to Beijing. We had already arranged to stay there a few days to spend time relaxing with friends. All the members of our group were going back, as well. Sainshand did not have an airport.

We boarded the train in the morning to head back to Ulaanbaatar.

Our trip back to Ulaanbaatar to catch our flight was uneventful. We shared a sleeping cabin with two strangers. With our broken Chinese and their broken English, we figured out arrangements for the "bunk" beds. They were much younger than we, and after a very animated discussion between themselves, they indicated we must take the lower bunks. (Bill and I were relieved as we weren't sure either of us could climb up to the top bunk.)

We spent another night in the Korean Guest House. Different room. A lidless toilet that had to be flushed by pulling up on a long wire attached to the flush mechanism. Two tiny towels. Beds as hard as the bare ground. I was actually looking forward to being back in a Beijing hotel! We had arranged to spend several days visiting friends and looking at the changes that had come with the Olympics. We were staying at the Lido, a lovely Western hotel with many wonderful restaurants.

The next morning, we headed for the Ulaanbaatar airport. It was cold and beginning to snow. We waited for what seemed like an eternity for a call for departure. It never came.

The airport at Ulaanbaatar had only one runway. If the weather and wind didn't cooperate, planes didn't fly in or out. We were told to come back the next day. Of course, we had no place to stay, having given up our places at the guest house. Much to our surprise, the airport authorities arranged for us to stay in a hotel at their expense. It was several steps up from the guest house. It had beds with western mattresses. The restaurant was good. We were able to reach one of our friends in Beijing. She took care of adjusting our hotel and contacting other friends.

The next morning it was back to the airport. Happily, the winds had changed and we were able to depart.

That night we met with friends at a restaurant in the Lido. It was great to reminisce about our times at NSCL. The school had grown and moved to a more western location. Unfortunately, it had encountered some financial problems and was forced to close a few years later.

CHAPTER 7

SARS

•

Ni fa shao le ma? (Knee fa shaow le ma) Do you have a fever today? Feidian (fay dee ann) SARS

THIS MEMOIR WOULD NOT BE COMPLETE WITHOUT A CHAPTER ABOUT living in China during the SARS epidemic. It colored our experience from December to May. We were relieved when government restrictions were finally lifted, but we continued on with some trepidation.

The Chinese government always plays its cards close to the vest. When SARs began in the country, the population was largely uninformed. We went home for Christmas and discovered from the news that there was a problem. It was said a virus had jumped from animals (bats) in an exotic food market in the Sichuan province and was spreading. A traveler from Sichuan had contracted the virus and taken it to Hong Kong. He had died from the illness. The WHO was concerned that China would not comment and denied anything worrisome was happening.

We returned to China to discover that the international health community had put pressure on the government and forced it to come clean. The disease was spreading everywhere. There was no cure.

Suddenly, the government took action. Local and international travel was shut down. People were in a tizzy. It was Chinese New Year, and no one was allowed to go to their hometowns to see family and celebrate. Public gathering places were closed. Many Beijing universities were closed and students/teachers quarantined behind gates manned by armed soldiers. If a case was found in an apartment, the building was quarantined. No one could go in or out. Family could drop off food and medicines at the gate in the hope the guards would take it to the sick. The father of one of our teachers came down with the illness. She took supplies to the apartment building every week. Ultimately, he suffered a heart attack, and he and his wife were taken to the hospital.

Whole hospital wings became SARs wings. Then entire hospitals. People who came down will the illness were reported to the authorities, who sent heavily guarded ambulances to take them away. Families could not go to the hospitals to help their sick relatives, as was the normal sick-caregiving requirement. Doctors and nurses were quarantined at the hospitals. They worked 12-hour shifts, in layers of gowns and gloves, as well as masks to try to keep themselves safe from the virus. They were diapered, as there was no time to stop for bathroom breaks. At the end of their shift, they would peel out of the layers of clothing and shower, eat, and go to sleep. Then they would start all over again.

The city of 14 million souls became a ghost town overnight. Normally sardine-crowded buses were empty. The streets were empty. The few people out were masked and avoided contact with one another. Public recreation facilities were closed, as were many restaurants.

The government closed schools, then put pressure on the international community to do the same. Heads of all the international schools met in the Canadian Embassy on a chilly morning to discuss what our approach would be. We determined we would do all in our power to help staff and families to be safe. That included providing thermometers and masks to all. Buses would be cleaned thoroughly with bleach each morning before they went to pick up the students, and then cleaned again when they arrived at the school. Our administrative/medical staff would be at the doors each morning to ask entrants "Ni fa shao le ma? and take their temperature. Anyone with a temp would be sent home. We would instruct parents to keep sick children at home. The schools would be completely disinfected at the end of each day. There would be a "No Visitors" policy. We presented our case to the Chinese government. They agreed but added to the agreement that any case or suspected case of SARs was to be reported immediately. We stayed open. Not one international school student or staff member developed a case of SARs.

I sent regular reports to our local newspaper in Colorado about SARs and it's progression in China, in particular in Beijing. Below is the text of those reports.

LIVING WITH SARS 2003

Feidian (fay dee ann) SARS

First News

Guangdong. A distant murmur of danger. "Faraway places with strange sounding names. . ." Even as close as Beijing, where my husband and I are living, China's vastness pushes concern a world away from my busy life. Guangdong. Strange habits and customs viewed through the two-dimensional lens of my tourist's eye. Some kind of illness resulting in the deaths of a few rural people. Probably some kind of Asian flu. Nothing really to do with me; more like a vapor or a mirage that dissolves when more important matters fill the mind. I think to myself, "What a shame," and turn my thoughts to what seem to be more essential concerns. A new home furnishings store has opened near our apartment complex. We discuss getting some patio chairs and a bookcase. I think about buying some potted plants to set out on the porch in the spring. I'm so tired of winter's chill, Beijing's gray signature buildings matted against the pale gray sky.

Rumblings

We are beginning to hear more of the illness in Guangdong. A growing rumor. Deaths and the threat of contagion. In passing, I wonder what is going on. Nothing from the Chinese government or its controlled press but the usual empty rhetoric and assurances. We refocus our thoughts on the day to day— Chinese lessons, school, the challenges of negotiating our way to and from jobs, stores, meetings. We talk about going to Hong Xiao or the Silk Market to purchase leather jackets and beaded purses and pearls. The flood of news reports about the prospect of war between the United States and Iraq commands our attention on the world news front.

On February 28, my school has its Valley Forge/Long March. We walk all day, a K-12 army, and eat corn cakes and gruel to commemorate the struggles of people to be free. Sungbin reads the Gettysburg Address; Chika recites King's "I Have A Dream"; and the 7th graders do a choral recitation of John F. Kennedy's Inaugural Speech. We all sing "Passing Through" and complain about the cold and the awful food.

"Wars and Rumors of Wars"

More reports of a growing threat are rumbling through our lives. Something virulent is marching unchecked through Guangdong. The foreign press reports tell us about a coronavirus called SARS, Severe Acute Respiratory Syndrome that has snared many and killed several. War has broken out between the U.S. and Iraq and I wonder, "Can it be Saddam has made good on his promise to unleash pandemonium on the world?" A doctor who was treating the sick in Guangdong has flown to Hong Kong and come down with the virus. China still discounts the significance of the illness. No one in Beijing is sick.

My father becomes critically ill and we fly to the states in a panic. In hospital rooms, on television news, we are confronted by growing coverage that indicates a significant health problem is developing in China. "Don't go back," our families and friends urge when the family crisis has ended with a positive result. But we return, certain that the press coverage is a tempest in a teapot that will soon blow itself out.

Nevertheless, I institute a rigorous anti-infection program at school and on the buses. We increase floor, bathroom, doorknob, banister, bus, lunchroom sanitizing to three times a day. We buy air hand dryers, and scrub hands frequently. We begin to screen visitors. All international schools begin to confer with one another about proactive strategies to allay parent, student and staff concerns.

Hong Kong is reporting cases of the illness. The Beijing municipal government assures the population that no one here is sick.

"April is the Cruelest Month"

My friend's daughter called today from Hong Kong where she and her husband work at an international school. Hong Kong is a city crippled by the SARS outbreak. She and her family have been holed up in their apartment for two weeks, too fearful to join the uneasy and potentially contagious masses on the streets. She is having food and water delivered. She has pulled her two children out of school. They are doing everything at homeschooling, recreating and living in four small rooms. They are afraid to come to Beijing, afraid they will somehow infect those they love, although they are not sick themselves. Every day she checks each family member for fever and watches for deadly symptoms.

I have become increasingly attentive, but Hong Kong is still far away. Nothing on the streets of Beijing suggests we need to be fearful. I reassure anxious parents and staff. "If this so called 'epidemic' has infected less than1000 people worldwide, what do we have to fear? We're living in a city of 14 million. There's more likelihood of being hit by a truck than of contracting SARS. And that certainly appears to be true. The streets of Beijing are wall to wall with bikes and buses, trucks and taxies, mule carts, cars, pedicabs and pedestrians. A friend of mine stepped off the curb last year and was run over by a passing bus. Her foot was crushed and recovery has been slow.

But life is good. Spring has finally arrived on Gobi wings. The magnolias, forsythia and lilac paint the breeze with their fragrance. The guards at our complex have changed from their long wool winter coats to lighter summer uniforms. The school's Science Fair is a huge success.

Countdown at Fourteen Days

SARS has come to town. A handful of cases have been reported among travelers from Hong Kong and southern China. A Finnish man has died; a Canadian is hospitalized. We are hearing rumblings of words like quarantine, isolation, probable and confirmed cases and "N95'. A few people on the street are beginning to wear masks. The World Health Organization WHO is asking questions and it is rumored that the answers they have been given may be untruthful. Our Board directs us to continue taking precautions.

At Twelve Days

The WHO has criticized China for attempting to cover up the growing problem in Beijing and elsewhere. The government has promised to come clean and suddenly the numbers of suspected and actual SARS cases have burgeoned. Beijing's SARS cases have jumped from a handful to a hundred. Rumors are flying - universities are rumored to be closing as cases are discovered on campuses; Beijing authorities are rumored to have hidden SARS cases in ambulances to keep the WHO from discovering them; whole planeloads of people are said to have been infected! I continue to sift through the information looking for rationality. The worldwide reports top 1,000. Still a small number. Every day we listen to the news, read the news, and speculate. My husband and I begin to talk about the possibility of leaving if the situation deteriorates. We consider if any of the "things" we just can't live without is more valuable than just going on living. We make jokes with our friends about not coughing and laugh nervously about being cavalier about a serious problem, looking furtively over our shoulders as if we know that the villain may be lurking at our elbow.

At Nine Days

The number of cases, suspected and confirmed, has tripled. The death count has risen to19. More masks on the street each day—from about 1 in 50 people to 1 in 10, then 1 in 5. Schools will not admit sick kids and absentees are closely monitored for symptoms. Ridership on public buses has dropped off. Buses that were standing room only a few days ago are populated by a small, masked population sitting in every other seat. The glut of cars, bikes, trucks, buses and pedestrians on the roads has dwindled. Traffic jams are no longer a problem; many fewer cars on the roads and both of us get to work in record time. Tourism has fallen sharply. My husband and I go to the big tourist markets and have a wonderful time. They are empty and the hawkers are eager enough for a sale to drop their prices to our desires.

At Seven Days

The numbers have risen again. I believe the government is just playing "catch up", not wanting to throw the true accounting out there all at once, but easing up to it. We are above 300, 200+ suspected. Deaths stand at 29. Three hospitals, Ditan, XieXi and People's Union have been designated for use by expats. I think to myself that is a lot of hospital beds and there are only about 100,000 expats in Beijing. Does this mean they are bracing for disaster? Still, I tell myself and others "500 of 14 million". There is no reason to panic. We are relatively certain it's a contact disease. If it were infectious, there would be no hope. We'd all be infected by now. We will increase our measures to maintain a controlled environment for the school and we'll all be fine. We check on all absences daily. No one may come to school if they have a fever or any of the other SARS symptoms until they have seen a doctor.

I pray the Board and I have not erred in our thinking. The lives of many people at my school will depend on clear thinking and definitive action. If we are wrong, the consequences for others could be severe. I sit up in my living room and try to find the answers in the still, dark air.

At Five Days

The Chinese government announced today that it is canceling the Golden Week holiday to discourage travel and curb the spread of the disease. In response, thousands begin to flee the city; foreigners to their own countries, locals back to their hometowns and mom. I would like to go home to my mom. Even while I look at the situation rationally and logically and know the risk of contracting SARS is slight, there is a tiny knot of terror in my heart. Like a tumor, almost imperceptible, but deadly.

At Four

We closed the school today. Workers at the university with which we are collocated were exposed to a SARS infected individual in their apartment building. They have been at work since the exposure although they have presented with no symptoms. The university has closed; everyone has been sent home under observation. While

the most current medical information on SARS convinces me
that our community is not at high risk, caution closes us down
to wait out the 10-day incubation period. I meet with the staff
before school to tell them the news and the steps that need to be
taken to provide for the students over the next two weeks. I am
met with frightened eyes and pallid faces, but they are seasoned
professionals and complete their tasks with courage, never allowing
their personal fears to infect the children. Even on this terrible day,
laughter, bustle and song emanate from the classrooms.

Three

I have been up most of the night fielding anxious phone calls
about developments and rumors. Someone calls to tell me not
to go to the office in the morning because all SARS patients
are being transferred to special hospitals and the air quality will
be extremely dangerous. As serious as the situation is, it's hard
not to laugh at this one!

At four in the morning, my Executive Assistant calls in tears.
She has been quarantined for 10 days. She is convinced she will
become ill and has infected the rest of us. The girlfriend of the
driver of the public bus she rides has been confirmed to have
SARS. We talk until she calms and agrees that it is unlikely she
will get sick. But she hangs up with a goodbye still ragged with
fear. Other office staff call and express their fear of going to the
office in the morning. The librarian calls to tell me not to go in
until she can disinfect everything. We both arrive at 8:30 and
go through the process, then settle in for the day.

A teacher's parents have had a close encounter with SARS and remain at high risk. Her father has been in the intensive care unit at a local hospital. He is still quite ill. Today his wife discovered that a patient in the same unit has been diagnosed with SARS. The teacher's father is too ill to go home, and the hospital refuses to move him to another floor. Pregnant herself, she cannot risk going to the hospital. She makes phone call after phone call trying to get help. The doctor hangs up on her. Her mother tells her that orderlies and nurses are fleeing the facility. Finally, she finds an advocate who will go to the hospital and petition for the removal of her parents to safety.

I attend a Beijing Education Commission meeting with all international school heads. The Chinese are closing all primary and secondary schools for two weeks and strongly suggest we do the same to try to monitor the situation. There have been 135 cases reported in Beijing schools—children and staff—over half at the university level. No deaths have been reported. No cases have occurred in international schools. When I return to school, I compose an information update to parents and staff, then head home. My thoughts stray to whether my husband and I can get masks.

Yesterday

The rumble has become a roar. The roar of airplanes and trains filled with frightened people fleeing to their distant homes. The roar of crowds emptying supermarket shelves. The roar of angry citizens condemning the government's poor handling of the situation. The roar of rumors about the possible quarantining of the city, martial law, forced isolation.

Beijingers are now masked – 3 in 5 people. The cotton and gauze varieties can be purchased on the street. Beijing Family United Hospital is selling the real deal for 40 quai at the hospital, which is a virtual ghost town. I have developed a runny nose and sore throat and call my doctor. Dr. Gee says that SARS doesn't usually present with a runny nose, but if I develop a fever to call him back. He says that there is little business at the hospital beyond phone calls. Expats are afraid to appear at any hospital for fear an errant cough will send them into isolation, or worse that they might be exposed to an infected person.

Our Chinese tutor called this morning. Her husband attends one of the local universities. It has been closed and all staff and students are quarantined on the cordoned off campus. She and her 8-year-old daughter can only wait and hope. She doesn't think it's wise to have a lesson today. She's nervous, worried about her husband and worried about her job. She works for a company that provides crash courses to foreigners in Mandarin. Business has come almost to a standstill.

We hear that the government is cordoning off infected buildings in an effort to contain the virus. Although we live in Haidian, the most impacted district in the city, I have not seen this. Consider the fact that there are probably a million buildings in Beijing; the chances of seeing a handful of roped off and guarded structures is not great.

May 1, 2003

The streets of Beijing are nearly deserted. Buses once packed like sardine tins have a few masked passengers. Taxi drivers ask us to write our name, address and phone number on a sheet they carry with them. They are turning these in at the end of each day to register their contacts. Feidian has free reign. A 1000 bed hospital was built north of us in Chaoping in a week's time. Already 150 victims have been transferred to the facility from city hospitals. The numbers of suspected and actual cases is growing—over 3,000. It is rumored that 20,000 are quarantined. Haidian district, where we live, has over 500 cases.

I receive a faxed directive from the Beijing Education Commission. It says that we must set up a quarantine facility on our campus to isolate suspected and SARS cases. It is to be our responsibility to staff the facility and shoulder the cost. This flies in the face of an earlier document that dictated that international schools were able to report such cases to the government and require home quarantine for suspected cases. I contact the liaison for international schools for guidance, explaining that international schools are not boarding schools and have no facilities to comply with such a directive. I know that if we are forced to comply with this directive, we will have no choice but to close for the balance of the year. Not even the giants like ISB and WAB can bear the cost of such a step. Parents would leave more quickly than they are now. In all schools, enrollment has nose-dived. Nervous families continue to return to home countries. Schools have lost around 14% of their population.

Ultimately the Commission agrees that the directive should have indicated that international schools were exempt from establishing a quarantine facility. Our Board still supports keeping the school open. So, life goes on. I am in the process to locating thermometers (virtually impossible to find in China now), an automatic digital thermometer to check everyone who comes into school when we reopen on May 12, enough N95 masks for the school and parent population, disposable gloves, antiseptic hand cleaner, antibacterial soap, and bleach for our stand off against SARS.

No one from my school is currently ill. No one is quarantined. Nor have I encountered anyone who has contracted SARS, is recovering from SARS or knows anyone with SARS. Yet as I pass an older couple on the street, I cannot help but wonder, "Will you still be alive a month from now? Will I?"

May 7

Julia and Lois have returned to work. Neither has contracted SARS, but both have been on edge today. Lois was never really at risk, but because Julia had been tangentially exposed and because Lois, who has lupus, works closely with her, she was terrified and stayed home for 10 days. I give each a box of disinfectant wipes and explain that they can use them to clean off their desks, phones, computers, chairs and cabinets. We talk about the health plan we will initiate on Monday and who will sit each day at the screening table. We plan a meeting with administrative staff on Friday morning, one with teachers in the afternoon, one with bus drivers and Ayi's on Sunday morning. Everyone has to know the role they will play and have the equipment they will need to carry out their duties. Drivers, screening table people and Ayi's will be the front line. They will face the most risk of exposure to the unknown; the Ayi's from their cleaning tasks, the drivers and screeners from possible carriers.

May 9

We set up the screening table schedule. Julia and I will be the first screeners each morning. All children and staff will be checked through by us each morning. Xue Xue, our librarian, will take the next slot, followed by Lois, our accountant, Jon the former Head of School, and the copy Ayi to close out the day.

The teachers arrive at 10 although they are not scheduled until 1:30. Lots of nervous laughter; they are happy to be back, to have something constructive to do, to be out of their apartments. At 1:30 we review the plan, the cleaning procedures, how we will screen, which children will return, how we will deal with getting work to those who are afraid to do so. We conclude at 3:30, and everyone stays to get their classrooms ready to see children again. We will be at about 50% enrollment on Monday.

The University Head decides we must have passes for all staff and licenses for the cars of people's drivers. Julia spends the afternoon making and laminating them. The Head is very nervous about our return and tries to discourage me from opening. I know that in his mind he fears a case of SARS happening in a foreigner on his campus. It will be his fault and he will be held responsible. He thinks we should wait two more weeks like the Chinese schools. Finally, he defers to the decision of the Education Commission that international schools may open, but requests that we sign a paper saying we won't hold him responsible if one or our people get sick.

May 11

I meet with the drivers and Ayi's. I tell them how much we value their contribution to this fight. They know they are at high risk and express their appreciation that someone understands their bravery. I explain to the Ayi's why they must wear masks and gloves while cleaning to reduce their exposure to germs. Drivers will also be masked and gloved while driving and will have disinfectant cleaner and spray to prepare the buses for children each day.

It's Mother's Day. I think I would like to see my mother, and my kids and just enjoy the day with people I love. But perhaps my job this Mother's Day is to be a mother to many and to see to it that other mother's kids are protected from a menace. Perhaps that is the best thing I have ever done on Mother's Day - something to help many other mothers who love their kids as fiercely as I do mine, and who are entrusting their children to my care.

May 12

Julia and I sit masked and gloved at the table at the top of the stairs, waiting, looking official, and I'm certain, frightening. Slowly students begin to climb the stairs. I ask them frightening questions in Chinese: Did you have a fever when you got up this morning? Have you been around anyone who has SARS or is suspected of having SARS? Have you traveled in the last two weeks? Where? I press hand sanitizer onto their hands and ask them to rub it in. I try to lighten the atmosphere with some chit chat. "Did you miss us? We missed you. I think you grew two inches while you were gone". Julia takes the temperature of each. When they are cleared, we let them into the building. More begin to appear, and teachers. Same routine. By 8:35 all who are coming today have entered the doors and the first day of school begins.

At 9:15 we come together for a Welcome Back Assembly, complete with a discussion about the plan, their role and responsibility and the seriousness of the situation. We finish up with recognizing April and May birthdays, a rousing birthday song in English and Chinese and cookies sent by a parent who owns a bakery. We have half of our kids. More will come now, knowing that we have reopened; that their friends have come back. Many lives that we are responsible for protecting. I pray that SARS will not come for a visit.

Last Day

When the last day of school came, we cheered that we made it through the epidemic. Our numbers in attendance had returned to normal. No one got SARs. Parents kept sick children home and returned then to school when they were well again. Staff maintained their health, though we lost some Ai's and Bus drivers who had fled to the country and did not return. Just our administrative staff stayed on for the summer, and we hoped the illness would be gone when school resumed in the fall.

CHAPTER 8

Farewell to China

Zai jian (Zye jan) Good bye

I HAD A 3-YEAR CONTRACT WITH THE NSCL INTERNATIONAL School. I was not able to complete that commitment. Sadly, our adventure in China was cut short by my father's diagnosis of Parkinson's Disease. My mother was struggling and asked us to return to the States to help. We packed and sent most of our belongings home in June. Bill and I returned, as well, and Bill stayed. We began searching for a home that would accommodate us and my parents

I left Beijing as I found it, sweltering in the steamy summer, wallowing in people, the deafening metallic thrum of June Bugs. Sandal-footed women loudly talking with each other in harsh staccato. With their irritating, boisterous laughter. Men with their shirts pulled up around their chests; drivers sitting in jeepneys wiping the sweat streaming down their faces; everyone looking for a small patch of shade in which to sit and fan themselves; the old men sitting sandaled and bare-chested or in their undershirts playing Chinese checkers in the heat of the afternoon.

But my first impressions had changed. They were still unattractive men, slope shouldered, with brown teeth. Smokers with poor dental hygiene wearing thin, rust-brown cotton shirts that reminded me of polyester leisure suits, shirttails out, unstylish, short waisted looking like old men with their belts up too high, soft and no muscle definition, squatting flat footed in the dirt, smoking and talking. Walking with bellies protruding, hands behind their backs. But now Xin was my point of reference, and I adored and admired him.

There were still prattling women, whose tone and decibel level were fingernails scraping across the blackboard of my ears. But now Star came to mind and made me smile. Beautiful, graceful Star, who invested a great deal of time in teaching us Chinese culture and language.

I returned to Beijing in late July to fulfill my commitment to help prep for the new school year and assist with an HOS search. School resumed in early September with no issues, and at full enrollment. Our search for a new HOS had not produced a successor by October, when I was slated to leave. It was determined by the Board that the HOSE would serve as an interim until a new HOS could be secured.

I was ready to be done by that time in order to focus on helping my parents. We were able to purchase a perfect home to move into together. The home had a handicapped accessible "mother-in-law" apartment that gave them privacy and autonomy, while being in earshot of support and assistance. We started renovations on the apartment to enlarge it, open an entrance to the main house, and add a dishwasher and washer and dryer. We moved them in as the contractor was completing the final clean up.

A Pound of Sand

As we prepared to move back to the States, I packed my Gobi sand in a gallon freezer bag and put it in the bottom of my suitcase. I never gave it another thought. The authorities and the Beijing airport, however, opened my suitcase and removed the bag. There was a great deal of discussion among the officials. The bag was weighed and opened. The contents were felt, smelled and tasted. I talked through the entire process, in English, of course, but with plenty of gestures, and finally my sand was put back in my suitcase and I was allowed to take it with me. Back in the States, I filled intricately carved oriental boxes with Gobi sand and gave them as Christmas gifts. I kept one for myself, of course, and I still take it out and look at it and marvel that it is actual sand from the Gobi Desert. Along with my camel bells, it is one of my greatest treasures.

You may be wondering what I did with my camel hair. I still have it too, by a miracle of ignorance. It wasn't until we got back to the States that I realized a had a plastic bag full of camel hair in my suitcase, in addition to the sand. It never occurred to me to declare it. I'm sure it would have been confiscated if it had been noticed. I still keep the raw camel wool with my cashmere wool and my loom.

Returning to the States

Mei guanxi (may guan she) No problem

The goodbye parties were over. My friends and colleagues sent me off with lovely gifts to remind me of our times together, including a beautiful batik wrap, an exquisite jewelry carrier, and a painting by a local artist. My office was cleaned out. I was packed. I had my tickets. I was ready to head out for the airport, and my driver was scheduled to pick me up.

On the day of my departure, I dropped the apartment keys on the dining room table, locked the door, and pulled my suitcases to the front porch. Our doorman rushed up the four stairs to assist me. As he eagerly reached for the luggage, he inadvertently ran into me and knocked me backwards off the porch. It was only about a 3-foot fall, but I fell hard on my arm and shoulder. Ouch!

The doorman was beside himself. Poor thing. I wanted to jump right up, but I didn't feel strong enough to do so. I just kept patting his hand and saying "mei guanxi" – no problem.

My driver arrived and jumped out of his car. He and the doorman picked me up and gently dusted me off. My driver wanted to take me to the hospital, but I assured him I was fine - mei guanxi again. I made him take me to the airport. I wasn't quite as fine as I had asserted, and I knew it. I spent 10 miserable hours flying home, sick to my stomach, feverish and in pain; but I was ready to be home. I didn't want to have to stay another day in China or deal with the problems that would have arisen from having to change my ticket. I went to the doctor when I got home. Nothing was broken, just pulled and sprained, thank goodness.

Farewell and Thank You

China will not notice that I'm gone. But the taxi drivers will wonder perhaps, where is that woman that lived on Xi San Qi? And the girls at the markets might ask, off handedly, whatever happened to me. My greengrocer will stop ordering lettuce. In a city of 14 million, you are a speck of dust, a struggling shrimp in a wriggling heap. I like to think I made some inroads, though, if only in a few lives. NSCL was better organized. Its image was significantly improved. Staff had become a cohesive and productive group. I think the kids got a better education and experience. I hope my Chinese friends are better for having known me.

I am certainly changed. I have grown more aware of my personal biases. I learned to live in a very different culture than my own. The acquisition of another language expands one's understanding of a different culture. And I think I was called upon to "put your money where your mouth is".

In China, I was an immigrant. I was struggling. I had no frame of reference. Nothing was familiar. I couldn't even read signs or labels. We couldn't join a church. Expat community groups were an hour away on the west side of town. If there were Chinese groups, we didn't speak Chinese wall enough to jump in, nor were we approached and invited. It was hard to fit in outside of the workplace, hard to get to know people, hard to become part of a neighborhood community. We were 2 nobodies in a very large somebody pond. It was a humbling experience. But I'm glad I was able to learn what life is like when you are at the bottom of the pecking order.

I have always sympathized with immigrants. I remember when my sister-in-law came here from the Philippines. It was hard for her, and she spoke English. She was my hero – she was like a pilgrim, coming here and leaving her support system, her family and friends to build a new life in an unfamiliar place.

I would not return to China to live. It's simply too overwhelming. But I'm glad we jumped in and took it on. We were able to survive. We saw places we never dreamed of seeing – the Great Wall, the Peking Man site. We met some amazing people from many lands – China, the US, India, Pakistan, Canada. We were immersed in Chinese culture – the opera, the massage, moon cakes, the meat market.

And finally, I am so glad we learned the answers to all the important questions – "Fourteen million people? "Where does all the p—p go?"; "Why won't anyone sit by us on the qing gui?"; "Who in the world would eat cuttlefish pizza?"; and "Would you please help me scrape the red bean paste out of these rolls?"

Printed in the United States
by Baker & Taylor Publisher Services